National Forest Walks

Brian Conduit

© Brian Conduit, 2016

All Rights Reserved. No part of this publication may be reproduced, stored in a retrieval system, or transmitted in any form or by any means – electronic, mechanical, photocopying, recording, or otherwise – without prior written permission from the publisher or a licence permitting restricted copying issued by the Copyright Licensing Agency, 90 Tottenham Court Road, London W1P 0LA. This book may not be lent, resold, hired out or otherwise disposed of by trade in any form of binding or cover other than that in which it is published, without the prior consent of the publisher.

Moral Rights: The author has asserted his moral right to be identified as the Author of this Work.

Published by Sigma Leisure – an imprint of Sigma Press, Stobart House, Pontyclerc, Penybanc Road, Ammanford, Carmarthenshire SA18 3HP.

British Library Cataloguing in Publication Data
A CIP record for this book is available from the British Library.

ISBN: 978-1-91075-805-2

Typesetting and Design by: Sigma Press, Ammanford.

Cover photograph: View over the Trent valley from Battlestead Hill © Brian Conduit

Photographs: © Brian Conduit

Maps: Sigma Press

Printed by: Akcent Media

Disclaimer: the information in this book is given in good faith and is believed to be correct at the time of publication. No responsibility is accepted by either the author or publisher for errors or omissions, or for any loss or injury however caused. Only you can judge your own fitness, competence and experience. Do not rely solely on sketch maps for navigation: we strongly recommend the use of appropriate Ordnance Survey (or equivalent) maps.

FOREWORD
by John Everitt, Chief Executive, the National Forest Company

Walking is one of those things that captures the spirit of the place; the sights and sounds, the rise and fall of the landscape, and the feel of the elements. This book showcases twenty walks that help to capture the spirit of The National Forest and what makes it so special. Of course, you can find more imposing landscapes or more quaint villages across other parts of England, but I would challenge anyone to find another place that has been so dramatically transformed. In 25 short years a small miracle has happened across this 200 square miles of the Midlands. Without great fanfare, 8.5 million trees have been planted and 70km^2 of new woodlands and other habitats have been created, as a new forest for the nation has quietly appeared. Forest cover has increased from just 6% to an impressive 20% of the land area, and new access routes opened up for people to enjoy.

The walks highlighted here wend their way through the wooded landscape that now connects the ancient forests of Needwood in Staffordshire to Charnwood in Leicestershire, heralding the achievements of the National Forest Company and its partners. With every twist and turn they take you through the rich and varied history of the Forest that will surprise and delight; from wildlife to wetlands, breweries to battlefields and historic houses to heritage. And if this whets your appetite, you might like to challenge yourself to walk all 75 miles of the new National Forest Way.

Whether you are a regular visitor, a resident or a casual walker I'd encourage you all to come and experience The National Forest. It is a welcoming and generous landscape, easy to get to and easy to get around. So take some time to walk and reconnect with the landscape here, not just for what it is now but also what it represents – transformation and inspiration – and capture your own spirit of the place.

John Everitt
www.nationalforest.org

LOCATIONS OF WALKS

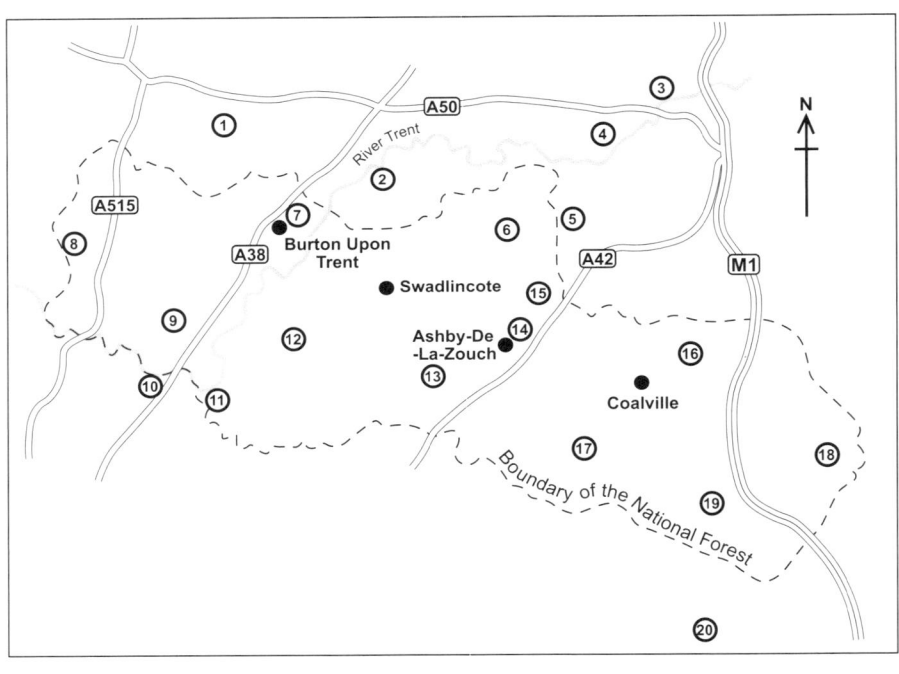

CONTENTS

Locations of Walks   4

Introduction   7

A Queen's Prison and a Wartime Disaster: 11
Tutbury, Stonepit Hills and Hanbury....7 miles (11.3 km)

Mercia's Ancient Capital: 17
Repton and Newton Solney....5 miles (8 km)

A Meeting of Three Waterways: 22
Shardlow, Derwent Mouth and Church Wilne....5 miles (8 km)

Walk Beside a Medieval Causeway: 27
Stanton by Bridge and Swarkestone....5½ miles (8.9 km)

Fine Views and Outstanding Churches: 32
Melbourne and Breedon on the Hill....6 miles (9.7 km)

A Baroque Mansion in Decline: 38
Calke Park....6½ miles (10.5 km)

A Rural Walk in a Town Centre: 43
Burton upon Trent....2½ miles (4 km)

A Fine Victorian Gothic Church: 47
Jackson's Bank and Hoar Cross....4½ miles (7.2 km)

Villages, Woodlands and Canal: 51
Barton-under-Needwood....8 miles (12.9 km)

A Waterside Ramble: 57
Fradley Junction and Alrewas....5½ miles (8.9 km)

A Poignant Tribute: 61
National Memorial Arboretum, Alrewas and Wychnor....5 miles (8 km)

A Forestry Transformation: 66
Rosliston and Coton in the Elms....3½ miles (5.6 km)

The Forest's Industrial Heritage: 71
Moira Furnace and the Ashby Canal....4½ miles (7.2 km)

Ivanhoe's Castle: 76
Ashby-de-la-Zouch, Blackfordby and Smisby....7 miles (11.3 km)

Hall, Church and Parkland: 81
Staunton Harold....5½ miles (8.9 km)

Medieval Ruins: 86
Grace Dieu Priory and Wood....2½ miles (4 km)

From Opencast Mine to Forest Park: 90
Sence Valley....7½ miles (12.1 km)

Home of the Nine Day Queen: 96
Bradgate Park and Swithland Wood....5 miles (8 km)

Views across The Water: 101
Thornton Reservoir and Stanton Under Bardon....5 miles (8 km)

Death of A King: 106
Bosworth Battlefield....3 miles (4.8 km)

INTRODUCTION

A landscape is not a static phenomenon. Landscapes are evolving all the time, some more than others. The National Forest is changing quicker than most and in its fairly short life – less than two decades – those changes are already apparent. But what is the National Forest and where exactly is it? These are undoubtedly the most commonly asked questions by people from outside the area.

Its geographical location is straightforward enough. It extends over roughly 200 square miles of east Staffordshire, south Derbyshire and west Leicestershire within an area bounded by the large cities of Stoke-on-Trent, Derby, Nottingham, Leicester and Birmingham. Within its borders are four main towns – Burton upon Trent, Swadlincote, Ashby-de-la-Zouch and Coalville – villages and smaller towns, historic sites, mature woodland, new plantations, parkland, farmland and a former coal mining area. The River Trent winds across the heart of it and for much of the way it is partnered – and occasionally joined – by the Trent and Mersey Canal. Both waterways provide much attractive walking.

The previous paragraph reveals that the National Forest is more than just an area of woodland but this is nothing new. Contrary to popular belief, this was true of the larger forests that in the Middle Ages covered around a third of the country. But the primary aim behind the National Forest project is to increase the tree cover in the area to around 33% and provide a patchwork of woods in what had become one of the least wooded parts of the country. Over the last few centuries many of the trees had been lost as a result of agricultural encroachment, industrial development, urban growth and the demands of two world wars.

As the newly planted woodlands grow and become merged with each other, they will ultimately create a physical link between the two medieval forests whose remains occupy the western and eastern fringes of the area. These are the forests of Needwood and Charnwood respectively. In the Middle Ages Needwood in east Staffordshire was a royal hunting forest, part of the Duchy of Lancaster, and covered most of the area roughly between Uttoxeter, Tutbury and Lichfield. It was very thickly wooded and noted for its fine oaks but from the 18th century onwards most of it was felled. Charnwood in west Leicestershire was never a royal forest but a chase, sometimes referred to as Charley Chase, whose hunting rights were owned jointly between various earls and local religious houses. It covered an area roughly between Leicester, Loughborough and Coalville but, unlike Needwood, was never thickly wooded. Much of its lower land comprised rough heath and the higher slopes – and Charnwood is a hilly region rising to over 900 feet – were and still are characterised by fern and gorse interspersed with craggy outcrops.

Another aim of the National Forest is to regenerate areas of industrial decline and dereliction and make them green and attractive again. Part of the region, around Ashby-de-la-Zouch and Coalville, became a coal mining area and a number of pits were sunk in the early 19th century. The mines and many of the ancillary industries have now closed down and since the creation of the National Forest, derelict industrial sites have been restored, coal waste has been landscaped and trees planted to create attractive recreational areas of wood, grassland and water. Visits to Donisthorpe Woodland Park near Ashby, Sence Valley Forest Park just to the south west of Coalville and the area around Thornton Reservoir vividly illustrate how much of the landscape has been transformed in a remarkably short time.

This walking guide is not just confined to the boundaries of the National Forest but also includes a number of interesting and attractive areas on its periphery. As with many parts of the country outside the national parks and other obvious honeypot tourist destinations, this is very much an understated and underrated area. The landscape is pleasant and undulating rather than spectacular, although there are plenty of extensive, sweeping and even dramatic views from some of the higher points in Needwood and Charnwood forests looking across the valleys of the Trent and some of its tributaries. A number of great parklands are dotted throughout the area – Bradgate, Melbourne, Staunton Harold and Calke – and these provide superb walking facilities, as well as the intrinsic historic appeal of the great houses themselves and their attendant churches. The many woodlands, both new and mature, are obviously among the major attractions for walkers as are paths across riverside meadows and along canal towpaths. In addition there are attractive villages, perhaps less well known and commercialised than their counterparts in many other parts of the country, and many sites of historic interest, most of which are featured in the selection of walks.

The extensive network of generally clear and well waymarked public rights of way is supplemented by a number of permissive paths created by – among others – the Staunton Harold Estate, National Trust and Severn Trent Water. Also there is public access to all the new woodlands planted through the

National Forest scheme. A recent addition to the walking opportunities available in the forest was the launching of the National Forest Way in 2014. This 75 mile (121 km) long distance path snakes its way across the forest from the National Memorial Arboretum in Staffordshire on its western edge to Beacon Hill Country Park in Leicestershire on the eastern fringes. The way embraces all the varied aspects of the forest's landscape and is well-waymarked throughout. Many stretches of it are covered by the walks in this book.

The forests and chases of the past were the preserves of monarchs and aristocrats. The National Forest is an evolving forest, a forest for the present and future, a forest that can be enjoyed by all. And the finest way to enjoy and appreciate it is on foot.

General Information

Useful Organisations
The National Forest Company, Bath Yard, Moira, Swadlincote, Derbyshire DE12 6BD Tel: 01283 551211 **enquiries@nationalforest.org** **www.nationalforest.org**

Ramblers' Association, 2nd Floor Camelford House, 87-90 Albert Embankment, London SE1 7TW Tel: 020 7339 8500 **ramblers@ramblers.org.uk**

National Trust, PO Box 574, Manvers, Rotherham S63 3FA Tel: 0844 800 1895 **enquiries@nationaltrust.org.uk**

English Heritage, The Engine House, Fire Fly Avenue, Swindon SN2 2EH Tel: 01793 414700 **customers@english-heritage.org.uk**

Public Transport
For information about bus and train services either phone Traveline on 0871 200 2233 or visit **www.traveline.org.uk**. Alternatively contact the local visitor information centre

Maps
The sketch maps are only a rough guide and you should always take with you the relevant Ordnance Survey map. The most useful of these are the Explorer maps and the vast majority of the walks in this guide, 17 out of the 20, are

covered by Explorer 245 (The National Forest). The other three are covered by Explorers 232 (Nuneaton & Tamworth), 246 (Loughborough) and 260 (Nottingham).

Local Tourist Information Centres

Ashby-de-la-Zouch Tel: 01530 411767 **ashby.tic@nwleicestershire.gov.uk**
www.nwleicestershire.gov.uk

Burton upon Trent Tel: 01283 508000 **tourism@eaststaffsbc.gov.uk**
www.enjoyeaststaffs.co.uk

Sharpe's Pottery Museum, Swadlincote Tel: 01283 222848
tic@sharpespotterymuseum.org.uk www.south-derbys.gov.uk/tourism

WALK 1
A Queen's Prison and a Wartime Disaster:
Tutbury, Stonepit Hills and Hanbury

From the higher points on the route there are striking and extensive views across the Dove and Trent valleys and over the wooded slopes of Needwood Forest. There is also a variety of historic interest that includes the impressive Norman castle and priory at Tutbury, restored medieval church at Hanbury and the enormous crater near Hanbury that resulted from a mystery explosion during the Second World War.

Distance	7 miles (11.3 km)
Map	3½ hours
Starting point	Tutbury, top end of High Street, grid ref SK213288
Parking	Tutbury
Terrain	Riverside meadows, field paths and woodland, some modest climbs, over 25 stiles to negotiate
Refreshments	Pubs and cafes at Tutbury, pub at Hanbury
Public transport	Buses from Burton upon Trent, Derby and Uttoxeter
Map	OS Explorer 245 (The National Forest)

The Walk

The former glass making village of Tutbury is dominated by the extensive ruins of the Norman castle which crown a long ridge above the Dove valley. The castle was first built in the late 11th century and extensively rebuilt in the 12th century. In 1265 it became part of the Duchy of Lancaster and John of Gaunt, son of Edward III, added some walls and towers in the 14th century. Between 1569 and 1587 it served as the prison for Mary, Queen of Scots who hated the place, complaining that it was cold and damp. The castle fell into ruin after

Tutbury Castle

the Civil War and the great hall is the only part that has a roof and is still intact. The tower on the motte is a folly, added in the 18th century.

Just below the castle is the former Benedictine priory. Tutbury was one of a number of alien priories in England, which means that it was a dependency of a continental monastery, in this case an abbey in Normandy. It was dissolved by Henry VIII in 1537 and all that remains is the fine Norman church, much reduced in size.

Norman priory at Tutbury

1. Facing down High Street, turn left along Duke Street and continue uphill along Castle Street. At a public footpath sign just after the road bends left, turn right along an enclosed path. Immediately there is a striking view ahead over the Dove valley. Descend a flight of steps, go through a kissing gate, continue down beside the castle mound on the right and keep straight ahead across a meadow.

On the far side bear right through a hedge gap and turn left over a stile. Walk across a field, climb two stiles in quick succession and bear left across the corner of the next field to climb another stile. Maintain the same direction across a meadow – the River Dove is just to the right – keeping to the left of a ruined barn and gradually veering left to a stile at a hedge corner. Climb it and another one, walk along a left field edge and climb two more stiles in quick succession. Continue along the left edge of a field to a track, turn left over a stile, turn right to a road and turn right along it.

2. At a public footpath sign, turn left along a tarmac drive through Fauld Industrial Park. Bear right and just beyond a gateway, look out for where you turn right over a stile and walk along the right edge of a field. Climb a stile in the corner and turn left onto an enclosed path. Climb a stile, bear right though a gate, continue along an enclosed path and climb another stile. Bear slightly right and head steeply uphill over the Stonepit Hills, keeping to the left of the trees to reach the brow. This is a magnificent viewpoint over Needwood Forest and the Trent and Dove valleys, with the hills of the Peak District visible on the horizon.

From the brow follow a line of waymarked posts over bumpy ground to a stile on the edge of Queen's Purse Wood. Climb it and continue along a winding fence-lined path through this beautiful woodland to reach a track. Turn right, follow the track as it curves left and at a fork, keep along the

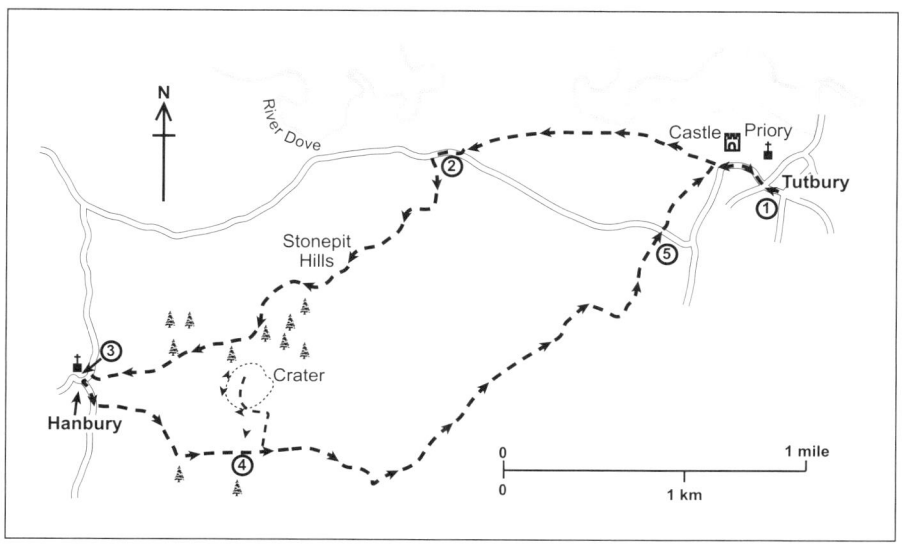

left hand track. At the next fork, take the left hand track and where the track bends right, keep ahead along a path, passing several notices on the left with warnings about unexploded bombs and steep drops. This indicates that you are near the edge of the crater but more about this later.

River Dove near Tutbury

Climb steps and go through a kissing gate on the edge of the woodland. Walk along the right edge of the next two fields but in the second field, veer left away from the edge to go through a kissing gate. Continue along an enclosed path, go through a gate, almost immediately turn left through a kissing gate, turn right and head across to a stile beside a gate. After climbing it, walk along an enclosed track and go through a kissing gate onto a road in the village of Hanbury. The Cock Inn is to the right but the route continues to the left.

View from the Stonepit Hills

The pleasant village of Hanbury has fine views over the Dove valley and Needwood Forest. The medieval church was extensively restored and partially rebuilt in the 19th century. It has a memorial window to the 1944 disaster.

3. At a T-junction, turn left in the Anslow and Burton direction and turn left along an enclosed track which passes to the left of Hanbury Memorial Hall. Go through a kissing gate and as you continue along the track ahead, passing through two kissing gates, grand and extensive views open up over the Trent valley. After the second kissing gate, continue along the right edge of a field, in the corner turn left to keep along the field edge and go through a kissing gate.

4. The main route continues ahead but turn left along the left edge of the field for a short detour to the crater. Go through a kissing gate, keep along the edge of the next field, go through another kissing gate and keep ahead through bushes to the crater, bearing left by a wire fence on the right and continuing to a memorial stone.

On the morning of 27 November 1944 a huge explosion at a large RAF ammunitions dump of over 4000 explosives, stored in former gypsum mines here, rocked the surrounding area. Over 70 people were killed, a local farm was destroyed and there was much damage in nearby Hanbury, including the Cock Inn. The cause of the explosion remains a mystery to this day but it is one of the largest ever non-nuclear explosions. The enormous crater left behind is approximately 1000 yards long and 300 yards wide.

Memorial to a mystery wartime explosion

Retrace your steps to the main route (4) and turn left to head across the field. After going over a low brow, crossing two stiles in quick succession, veer right and make for the far right hand corner of the field where there is a waymarked footbridge. Cross it and turn right to continue along the right field edge. In the corner turn left and then right over a stile and keep along the left edge of the next field.

Climb two stiles in quick succession, walk along the left edge of a field, bear left to climb two more stiles in quick succession and keep ahead towards the end of a hedge. Go through a squeezer stile and continue towards a farm, by the hedge on the left, bending first right and then left to pass to the left of the farm buildings. At a fork take the right hand track and at a public footpath sign where the track bends right, climb a stile and keep ahead across a field, climbing several stiles and making for the far right hand corner where you join a track.

Bear left, walk along the right edge of a field and just after the field edge curves left, look out for where you turn right over a stile. Turn left to continue along a left field edge and on emerging onto a track by a squeezer stile, turn right through another squeezer stile to continue along the left field edge. Follow the field edge around a right bend, turn left over a stile, turn right along the right edge of a field and cross a plank footbridge into the next field. Turn left along its left edge and at a junction of paths by a footpath post, bear left to cross another plank footbridge and keep along the right edge of a field to a road.

5. Cross over, take the path opposite to the left of a house and go through a kissing gate. Walk along the left field edge and turn right to head uphill, keeping by the left edge of the field and pass through a hedge gap to a kissing gate. Go through, continue up to emerge onto a road in Tutbury and turn left. Where the road curves right downhill you pick up the outward route and retrace your steps to the start.

WALK 2
Mercia's Ancient Capital:
Repton and Newton Solney

Between Repton and Newton Solney there is attractive riverside walking beside the Trent, passing its confluence with the Dove. On the return stretch you leave the river to climb gently above the valley and are rewarded with some superb and extensive views across gently rolling countryside, with the spire of Repton church prominent.

Distance	5 miles (8 km)
Approx. time	2½ hours
Starting point	Repton, Market Cross, grid ref SK304270
Parking	Repton
Terrain	Easy walking across fields and riverside meadows
Refreshments	Pubs at Repton, pubs at Newton Solney
Public transport	Buses from Derby and Burton upon Trent
Map	OS Explorer 245 (The National Forest)

The Walk

For a short while Repton was the capital of Mercia and its church the burial place of Mercian kings. The town has quite a complicated ecclesiastical history. The church was founded in 653 and an adjacent monastery established shortly afterwards. It was sacked by the Danes in the winter of 873-4 but the 8th century crypt, intended to be the mausoleum of the Mercian kings, survived and lies under the present church which was built later on the monastic site. This church was substantially enlarged between the 13th and 15th centuries and the impressive tower and spire, 212 feet high and a landmark for miles around, dates from the 15th century.

Repton's imposing church

A Benedictine priory was founded in 1172 next to the church and the former Saxon monastery. This was dissolved by Henry VIII in the 1530s and a school was founded on the site in the reign of Elizabeth I. The arch from this former priory now forms the entrance to some of the school buildings. Repton School now totally dominates this small and unassuming town as almost every other building seems to be connected with it.

This arch is all that remains of a medieval priory at Repton

1. Facing the church, walk along the main road and follow it around left and right bends. Just after the right bend and at a sign for Science Priory, turn left onto a straight tarmac path, called Jeremiah's Walk. Keep to the left of the modern school science building and where the tarmac path ends,

cross a lane and keep ahead along an enclosed path to a stile. Climb it, head diagonally across an uneven narrow field, keep along its left edge to a hedge corner and continue across the field to climb a stile in the right hand corner. Keep ahead, by a hedge on the left and above a wooded hollow on the right, and follow the path to a gate. Go through, keep along the right field edge, by woodland on the right and climb a stile in the corner. Do not continue by the fence on the left but take the path ahead that heads gently down to the River Trent. Keep ahead by the river, go through a gate and the path later curves right through a hedge gap.

Immediately turn left to a waymark and keep ahead, picking up a hedgeline on the right. Look out for a fence corner where you turn right over a stile and turn left to continue with the hedge on the left. At the corner of the fence, keep ahead across the field, veering left and making

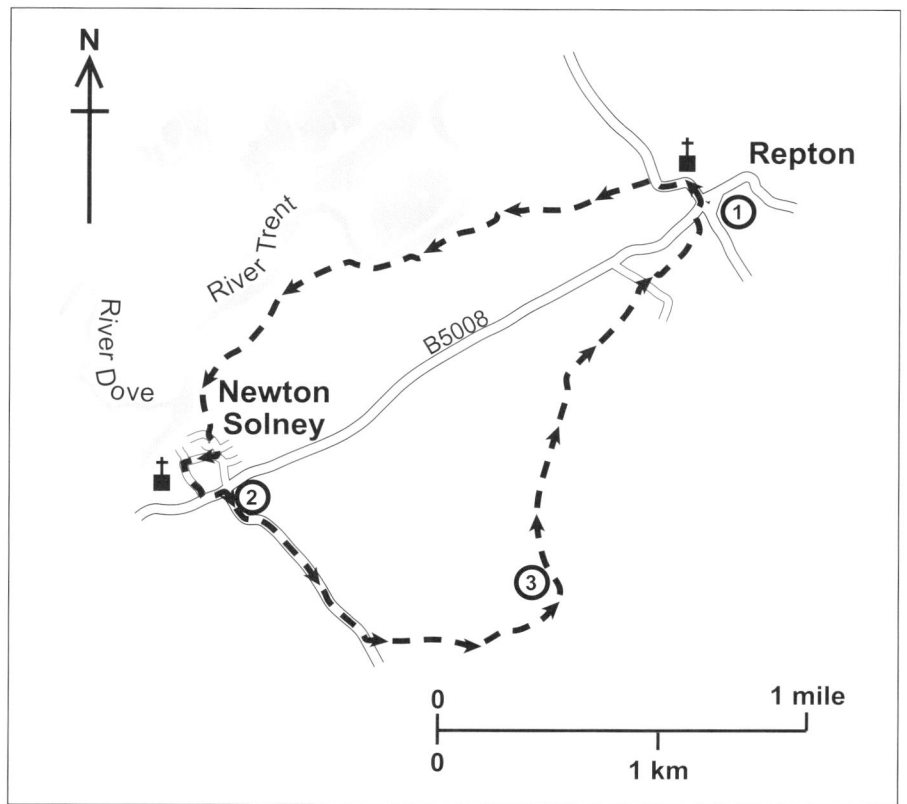

for a stile beside a gate in the fence on the left hand side of the field. After climbing it, bear right across the field corner to another gate and go through to rejoin the riverbank near the confluence of the Trent and Dove. Go through a gate, walk along a track, by a barn on the left, and where the track curves right, keep ahead across the grass to a stile. Climb it, continue across the next field, climb another stile, head across a playing field and go through a gap in the fence in the far left corner to emerge onto a road in the village of Newton Solney. Turn left, take the first road on the right (Blacksmiths Lane) and at a T-junction, climb the steps in front, walk along a path and go through a kissing gate into the churchyard.

Confluence of the rivers Trent and Dove at Newton Solney

The small village of Newton Solney occupies a delightful situation near the confluence of the Trent and Dove. Its fine medieval church was founded in the 12th century but mainly dates from the 14th and 15th centuries. There are some attractive Victorian almshouses in the main street.

Go through another kissing gate, turn left along a drive to a road and turn left again through the village.

Medieval church at Newton Solney

2. Take the first road on the right (Newton Lane, Bretby Lane) and after ½ mile (0.8 km), turn left along a tarmac, fence-lined drive. In front of the gates to a house, turn left through a gate, walk along the right field edge and go through a gate. Bear right across a field heading down into a dip, go through a gate, bear right and head gently uphill to a stile. Climb it, turn left along the left field edge and

climb another stile. Keep ahead across a field, passing to the left of a tree that marks an old hedgeline, and about halfway across the next field, look out for a path on the left and follow it in a straight line down to a stile.

3. Climb it, bear right to head across a large field, climb another stile on the far side, continue across the next field and go through a gate onto an enclosed track. Turn right and at a T-junction of tracks, keep ahead over a stile and walk across a field. Climb a stile in the corner, keep along the left edge of two fields, head straight across the next field and continue along an enclosed path to a road on the edge of Repton. Cross it, take the enclosed path opposite and follow it around a right bend to a stile. Climb it, keep along an enclosed path and pass beside a gate onto another road. Continue along an enclosed path and at a fork, take the left hand path to emerge onto a road. Turn right to the Market Cross.

WALK 3
A Meeting of Three Waterways:
Shardlow, Derwent Mouth and Church Wilne

The emphasis on this walk is very much on water. It starts at a fascinating former canal port and first takes you to the meeting place of three waterways: the rivers Trent and Derwent and the Trent and Mersey Canal. The lack of a footbridge over the canal at Derwent Mouth Lock means that there has to be some retracing of steps but this is no hardship as the wide views across the adjacent meadows are a more than adequate bonus and a visit to an isolated medieval church adds to the overall interest.

Trent and Mersey Canal at Shardlow

Distance	5 miles (8 km)
Approx. time	2½ hours
Starting point	Shardlow, Wharf car park, grid ref SK445305
Parking	Shardlow Wharf
Terrain	Flat walking along quiet lanes, across meadows and on a canal towpath
Refreshments	Pubs at Shardlow
Public transport	Buses from Derby and Loughborough
Map	OS Explorer 260 (Nottingham)

The Walk

1. Turn right out of the car park along the road and just before the canal bridge, turn left down steps, turn sharp right to pass under the bridge and walk along the towpath of the Trent and Mersey Canal, passing a marina on the left, to Derwent Mouth Lock. Continue for a further ¼ mile (400m) to Derwent Mouth.

Not only is Derwent Mouth a beautiful spot but it is also the meeting place of three waterways. Here both the River Derwent and the Trent and Mersey Canal flow into the broad waters of the River Trent. Downstream a viaduct takes the M1 motorway over the Trent.

2. Retrace your steps to the canal bridge at Shardlow, pass under it and continue along the towpath for an exploration of this attractive former canal port. Leave the canal at the next bridge and turn right over it. On the

Derwent Mouth, the meeting place of the Trent and Mersey Canal and rivers Trent and Derwent

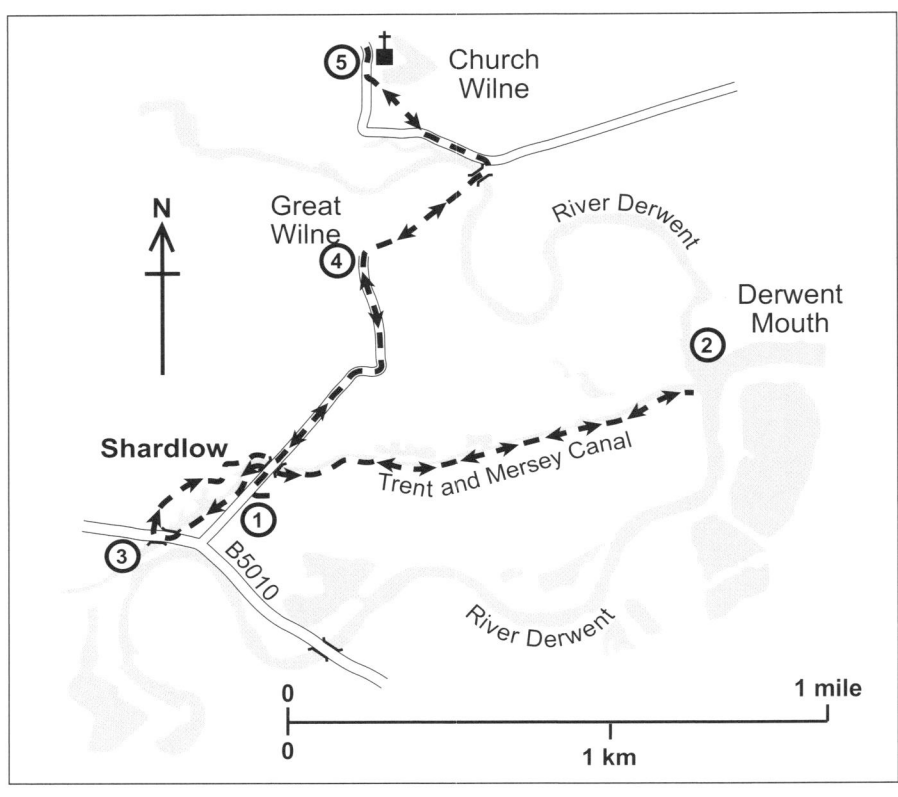

other side of the road are two of Shardlow's iconic canal buildings, the Heritage Centre and the Clock Warehouse, both housed in former warehouses.

Situated near the confluence of the rivers Trent and Derwent, the small river port of Shardlow grew rapidly after the opening of the Trent and Mersey Canal in 1777. The canal was constructed to link the Trent with the River Mersey at Runcorn in Cheshire, a distance of about 93 miles (149 km).

The decline of the canals led to Shardlow becoming almost derelict by the 1970s but since then conservation and restoration has led to its revival and there has been greater recognition of its unique place in the nation's history. It is a rare and fascinating example of an 18th century canal port with warehouses, wharves, cottages and houses, stables, boat building yards and other buildings associated with the canal trade at that time. Particularly impressive is the Clock Warehouse, built in 1780 and now a pub. It is so called because a clock once adorned the front of the building. The nearby Heritage Centre is housed in the oldest warehouse in the village and well worth a visit.

3. On the other side of the bridge turn right along The Wharf. Where the road ends, keep ahead along a short stretch of enclosed path to emerge onto a lane. Turn left, turn right at a junction and bear left beside the canal again to the bridge.

   Now comes a there and back walk to Church Wilne. Turn left at the bridge and follow the lane into the hamlet of Great Wilne. Follow the lane around right and left bends and continue to where it ends.

4. Climb a stile and turn right to follow a worn path across a field, keeping parallel to its right edge. At the far end, cross a footbridge over the River Derwent, turn left beside the river and the path emerges onto a lane. Turn left and at a public footpath sign, turn right and walk across a field. Go through a hedge gap, cross a track and continue along the right edge of the next field to a lane. Turn right to the church at Church Wilne.

Trent and Mersey Canal near Shardlow

Clock Warehouse at Shardlow

Isolated church at Church Wilne

The highly atmospheric church of St Chad stands in isolation on low lying land that has always been prone to flooding, hence the virtual disappearance of the village. The church dates back to the Middle Ages but had to be almost entirely rebuilt after being gutted by fire in 1917. Across the road is St Chad's Water, a local nature reserve reclaimed since 1984 from gravel workings, and a most attractive and tranquil place to relax before returning to Shardlow.

5. From the church retrace your steps to Shardlow and the starting point.

WALK 4
Walk Beside a Medieval Causeway:
Stanton by Bridge and Swarkestone

This varied walk includes two villages, two churches, the track of a former railway, a canal towpath and extensive views across the Trent valley. In many ways the highlight is the stretch beside the unique and impressive Swarkestone Causeway, about ¾ mile (1.2 km) in length, which has been a major routeway across the wide flood plain of the River Trent since the Middle Ages.

Distance	5½ miles (8.9 km)
Approx. time	2½ hours
Starting point	Stanton by Bridge, by the small triangular green, grid ref SK373273
Parking	Roadside parking in Stanton by Bridge
Terrain	Flat walking mainly across fields and along a disused railway track and canal towpath
Refreshments	Pub at Swarkestone
Public transport	Buses from Derby and Swadlincote
Map	OS Explorer 245 (The National Forest)

The Walk

The pleasant village of Stanton by Bridge is situated on a low brow above the Trent flood plain at the southern end of the Swarkestone Causeway. The small church, which is passed near the end of the walk, dates mainly from the 13th and 14th centuries but was heavily restored in the Victorian era.

1. With your back to the village street, turn right along the main road and at a public footpath sign, turn sharp left along a fence-lined tarmac track.

Just before the track curves slightly left, turn right through a waymarked gate and head gently uphill across a field, later veering right to keep along the right edge of woodland. Go through a gate, continue by the edge of the trees, go through another gate (just after passing an electricity pylon) and turn right along a broad track.

Keep along this track for the next ¾ mile (1.2 km). Just after passing a sign on the left to Holy Well and just before reaching a road in King's Newton, turn left, at a public footpath sign, and walk across a field, making for a fence corner. Continue by a wall on the right to the corner of the field and climb a stone stile onto a lane in front of a thatched cottage. Turn left, climb a stile, keep ahead and on entering a field, bear right across it to a stile. Climb it, keep in the same direction diagonally downhill across the field and in the far corner climb a stile onto a lane. Turn left and just before a bridge, turn left down a tarmac track to emerge onto the former track of the Derby to Ashby Railway.

This was known as the Melbourne Line and was opened in 1868 and finally closed down in 1980. During the Second World War it was used exclusively by the Army and played an important role in the build up to the Normandy landings in 1944.

River Trent near Swarkestone

2. Bear left along it, in the Derby direction, go through a gate and keep ahead to cross the bridge over the broad waters of the River Trent. Continue along the track and at a cycleway sign (just before the next bridge), bear left downhill, in the Derby direction again, pass beside a barrier and turn left onto the towpath of the Trent and Mersey Canal. Walk along the towpath for ¾ mile (1.2 km) as far as Bridge 12.

Peaceful scene on the Trent and Mersey Canal

28

The Trent and Mersey Canal was opened in 1777 and linked the River Trent at Shardlow in Derbyshire with the River Mersey at Runcorn in Cheshire, a distance of 93 miles (149 km).

3. Immediately after going under the bridge, turn first left and then immediately right down to a footpath post. Follow a path diagonally across a field, go through a hedge gap, continue in the same direction across the next field and on the far side bear left to join a track. Walk along it, cross a bridge over a ditch, keep ahead across a field, climb two stiles and continue across the next field. From here there is a fine view of the Swarkestone Pavilion.

The exact role of this impressive building is something of a mystery and the various names that it has been given – pavilion, summer house, grandstand – clearly illustrates this. The style suggests that it was built in the early 17th century and it was linked with the now vanished Swarkestone Hall. It is likely that the grassy enclosure in front of it was used for some kind of sporting events. After falling into ruin, the building has been restored in recent years as a holiday let.

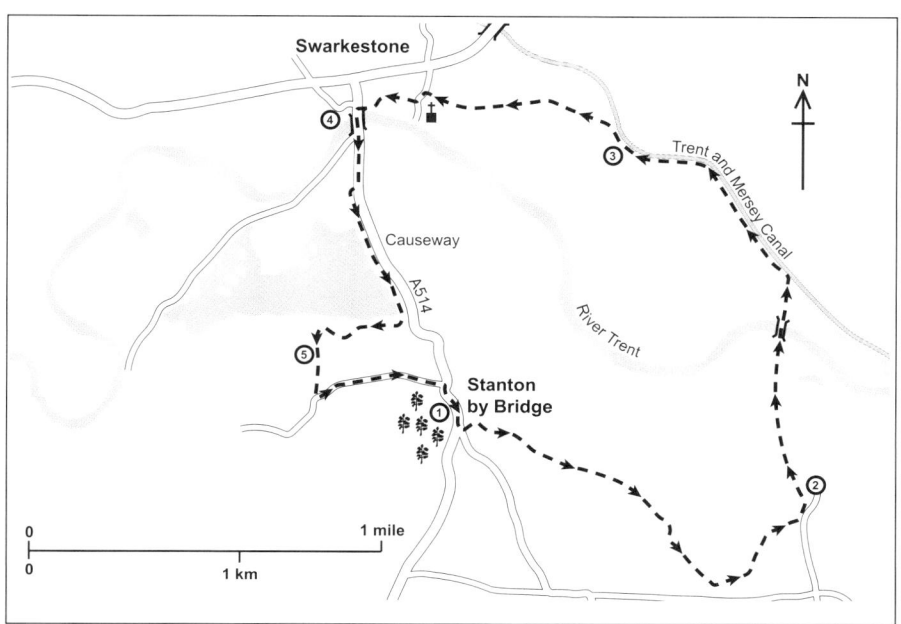

The Pavilion at Swarkestone

Nearby is Swarkestone church. Of medieval origins, it was mainly rebuilt in the 1870s.

Go through a wall gap, keep ahead by a wall enclosing the Pavilion on the right, turn left over a stile and turn right along a track. Do not follow the track to the right but keep ahead across a field (later by a wall on the left), turn left over a stile and turn right beside the churchyard wall to a lane. Turn left and opposite the gates of Swarkestone church, turn right onto a track. The track curves first left and then right and where it bends right again to a barn, keep ahead along an enclosed path. Continue by the left edge of a field, curving left and right. The River Trent is over to the left. Follow the path up to the main road opposite the Crewe and Harpur pub at Swarkestone, cross the road and turn left.

For centuries the bridge and causeway at Swarkestone was one of the principal crossings of the Trent and the main crossing between Derby and the south. It was first built in the 13th and 14th centuries but was widened several times in the 18th and 19th centuries. The bridge over the river itself had to be totally rebuilt at the end of the 18th century after being destroyed by floods. The total length of the bridge and causeway is ¾ mile (1.2 km), making it the longest stone bridge in the country. It was here in 1745 that Bonnie Prince Charlie and his Jacobite army halted on their march on London, turned back and returned to Scotland. There is a monument to this momentous event in the garden of the Crewe and Harpur pub.

Swarkestone Causeway

4. Cross the bridge over the Trent and continue along the causeway as far as a public footpath sign. Take care because the footpath is narrow and the road can be very busy. At the footpath sign, turn right over a stone stile, go through a gate and turn left. The next part of the walk is a fascinating stroll across the flood plain beside the causeway. Over to the right is the pool belonging to Swarkestone Sailing Club. Keep in a straight line, climbing two stiles, and at the end of the meadow, turn right, by a hedge on the left. After climbing a stile, continue along an enclosed grassy path, go through a gate, keep ahead and eventually the path bends left and crosses a footbridge over a ditch.

5. Keep ahead to a waymarked telegraph pole, bear slightly left and head gently uphill towards the houses of Stanton by Bridge on the brow. Climb two stiles in quick succession, bear slightly right across the next field, climb another stile and keep ahead to emerge onto a lane opposite Stanton church. Turn left through the village to return to the start.

WALK 5
Fine Views and Outstanding Churches:
Melbourne and Breedon on the Hill

There is much pleasant and easy walking across fields and through parkland with fine views over the surrounding countryside. Although the climb to the top of Breedon Hill is quite steep, it is short and well worth the effort both for the magnificent view and the interesting church whose tower can be seen for miles around. The final stretch beside The Pool, passing Melbourne Hall and the adjacent and exceptionally imposing Norman church, is particularly attractive.

Distance	6 miles (9.7 km)
Approx. time	3 hours
Starting point	Melbourne, Market Place, grid ref SK386253
Parking	Melbourne
Terrain	Field paths and tracks through gently rolling country, two climbs
Refreshments	Pubs and cafes at Melbourne, pub at Wilson, pub and cafe at Breedon on the Hill, tea room at Melbourne Hall
Public transport	Buses from Derby and Swadlincote
Map	OS Explorer 245 (The National Forest)

The Walk

Melbourne was once a centre for framework knitting and footwear manufacturing and possesses a number of attractive, brick-built Georgian and Victorian buildings. One of its most famous citizens was Thomas Cook, founder of the travel company, who was born here in 1808.

1. Start by walking along Church Street, passing to the left of the church, and the road continues as Blackwell Lane. At a public footpath sign, turn right

Superb view of Melbourne Hall and church from the footpath near the start

through a kissing gate and walk across grass. Keep by the edge of woodland on the right and bear left to a gate. Go through, bear left, head diagonally across a field and go through another gate. To the right is a magnificent view of the gardens adjoining Melbourne Hall, with the house and the church tower in the background. Continue in the same direction across the next field, bisecting two trees to reach a stile in a hedge. Climb it, head across the next field to a track on the far side and turn left beside a cattle grid. Bear slightly left, continue gently uphill along the left field edge and climb a stile on the brow. From here there are superb all round views. As you head downhill across the next

Hilltop church at Breedon on the Hill

33

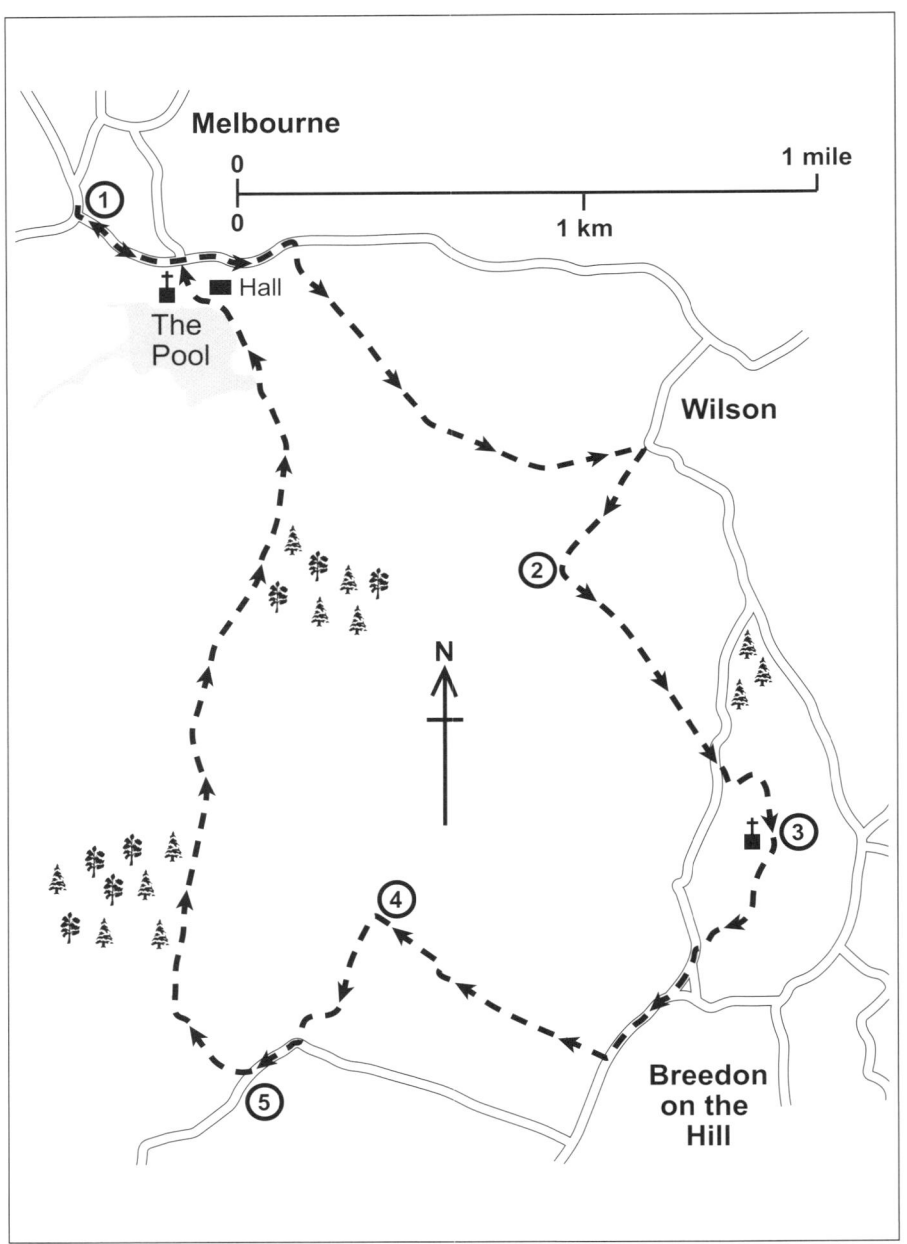

field, Breedon's hilltop church can be seen over to the right. The path emerges onto a road on the edge of the village of Wilson. The Bulls Head is a few yards to the left but the route continues to the right along a tarmac drive called Green Lane.

2. At a public footpath sign, turn left through a hedge gap and keep in a straight line across a golf course. There are several waymarked posts to show the way. Nearing the far end of the course, head across to the right edge and continue along a track under an avenue of trees. Where the track curves right, go through a kissing gate onto a narrow lane and take the path opposite. The path initially runs parallel to the lane but later bears left away from it and climbs steeply through trees to a lane. Turn left and the lane curves right to the church at Breedon on the Hill.

The isolated limestone bulk of Breedon Hill towers 400 feet (122m) above the surrounding countryside. The views are magnificent, extending over Charnwood Forest and the Trent valley to the cities of Derby and Nottingham. In clear conditions the southern fringes of the Peak District are visible on the northern horizon. Much of the eastern half of the hill has disappeared as a result of extensive quarrying activities.

The site is an ancient one with evidence of an Iron Age fort. In the 7th century a Saxon monastery was founded here. This was largely destroyed by the Danes during their conquest of Mercia but the Saxon heritage survives through the extensive collection of carvings built into the walls of the later medieval priory. Particularly impressive is the Breedon Angel, one of the earliest and finest surviving examples of Saxon sculpture. The priory was dissolved by Henry VIII in the 1530s and the present church is basically the tower and east end of that priory, purchased for the local people as their parish church by Francis Shirley of the nearby Staunton Harold Hall. The west end of the former priory was demolished because it was in such a bad state. As well as the Saxon carvings, the church contains some fine tombs of the Shirley family.

3. Where the lane ends, keep ahead through a gate and walk along an enclosed path which descends to a road in Breedon village. Bear right to a T-junction, turn left and where the road divides, take the right hand road across the green. Keep ahead along the main road and at a public footpath sign (just beyond the vehicle entrance to a garden centre), turn right onto a path through trees. The path curves left and then bends right to continue as a straight, hedge-lined grassy track. Continue by a hedge

on the left, go through a hedge gap and head gently uphill, still by a hedge on the left. Follow the field edge around first a right bend and then a left bend, head over the brow of the hill and, at a waymarked post, continue along a hedge-and tree-lined track. Again follow the track around a right bend and then turn left to descend into a dip and go through a hedge gap into a field. Turn left and follow the field edge to the right to a yellow waymark by another hedge gap.

4. Turn left first along an enclosed path and then along a right field edge. Follow the edge around right and left bends, pass beside a gate onto a lane and turn right.

5. At a public footpath sign, turn right over a stile, walk across a field and climb a waymarked stile in a fence. Bear right across a sloping field, go through a gate, turn left downhill and the path bends right to another stile. Climb it and walk along a path, later by the right edge of woodland, climbing a series of stiles. Later continue under an avenue of trees and soon the tower of Melbourne church comes into view. Where the track bends left towards a farm, keep ahead gently downhill, by a wire fence on the right, bending right to climb a stile in the field corner. Climb steps, walk along the right edge of the next field and where the edge curves right, keep ahead and climb another stile. Continue across a field to a stile in a hedge, climb it, head across the next field and go through a kissing gate. Turn left along a tarmac track for a most attractive finale along the right edge of The Pool and past Melbourne Hall and church to a road.

Melbourne church is unusually imposing for a small place, cathedral-like in dimensions and appearance and an outstanding example of Norman architecture. The most plausible reason for this is that it was originally a royal foundation, built by Henry I around 1120. In 1133 it was given by the King to the newly created bishopric of Carlisle. Almost the whole of the building dates from the early 12th century except for part of the chancel, rebuilt in the 15th century, and the upper part of the central tower, probably added in the early 17th century.

The adjacent hall was originally the rectory for the medieval bishops of Carlisle. It later came into the possession of the Coke family and was mostly rebuilt by them in the late 17th and early 18th centuries. The magnificent formal gardens were laid out roughly at the same time. During the first half of the 19th century it was the home of Lord Melbourne, Queen

Looking across The Pool to the tower of Melbourne's Norman church

Victoria's first Prime Minister, after whom the city of Melbourne in Australia is named.

At the road turn left to return to the Market Place.

WALK 6
A Baroque Mansion in Decline:
Calke Park

Focal point of this outstanding walk is a grand and unusual 18th century house. The first and last parts give you attractive and extensive views over Staunton Harold Reservoir and in between you stroll across the delightful and well-wooded parkland surrounding Calke Abbey, enjoying grand views of the great house and adjacent church.

Distance	6½ miles (10.5 km)
Approx. time	3½ hours
Starting point	Visitor Centre at northern end of Staunton Harold Reservoir, signposted from Melbourne, grid ref SK377245
Parking	Severn Trent Water car park at Staunton Harold Reservoir
Terrain	Gentle walking along field paths, through woodland and across parkland, over 20 stiles to negotiate
Refreshments	Tea room at Calke Abbey, pubs at Ticknall
Public transport	None to start but you could begin the walk from Ticknall which is served by buses from Nottingham, Swadlincote and Melbourne
Map	OS Explorer 245 (The National Forest)

The Walk

Staunton Harold Reservoir was created in 1964 and extends over an area of 209 acres. It has become an important wildlife habitat and a popular centre for water sports, fishing, bird watching, cycling and walking. The Windmill Tower, which overlooks the reservoir, was used for the milling of local grain. It was built in 1798 but had become derelict by the end of the 19th century. There is an information room at the visitor centre.

1. Begin by walking up to the Windmill Tower, pass to the left of it and at a public footpath sign, go through a fence gap, turn left to walk across a field, continuing along its right edge to a stile. Climb it and keep along the right edge of a new plantation (Broadstone Holt) created under The National Forest project. Climb a stile, continue along the right edge of the plantation and in the corner turn right over a stile. Walk along the left edge of a field, climb a stile and continue along an enclosed path by the left inside edge of trees, climb another stile and keep along a left field edge to a stile.

After climbing it, continue across a field, climb another stile, bear slightly left across the next field and climb a stile onto a lane. Cross over, climb the stile opposite and head down across a field to cross a footbridge. Keep ahead uphill across the next field and on the far side, turn left along the right field edge. It is at this path junction that the return leg joins the outward route. Continue along an enclosed path, re-entering the field, and walk across a corner of it to a stile. Climb it, cross a track, keep ahead

View over Staunton Harold Reservoir

39

across the next field and climb a stile in the corner. Keep ahead along the right edge of the next field but soon turn right through a gate to enter Calke Park.

2. Turn left along the left inside edge of woodland, go through a gate and continue beside the fence of a deer enclosure on the right. The path bends right, gently descends and continues through woodland to cross a footbridge over an arm of Staunton Harold Reservoir. Turn left across another footbridge and continue by the reservoir, crossing another footbridge.

The path eventually turns right away from the water and heads up to emerge onto a lane by a car park. From here there is a superb view looking towards the starting point at the northern end of the reservoir. Keep ahead along the lane and on the edge of Calke village, turn right along a tarmac drive. You pass to the left of the church and drop into a dip from where you get a magnificent view of the façade of the great house.

The splendid Baroque mansion of Calke Abbey is a vivid example of the decline of the English country house and is described in the National Trust's own leaflet as 'the un-stately home'. This is because its faded splendours

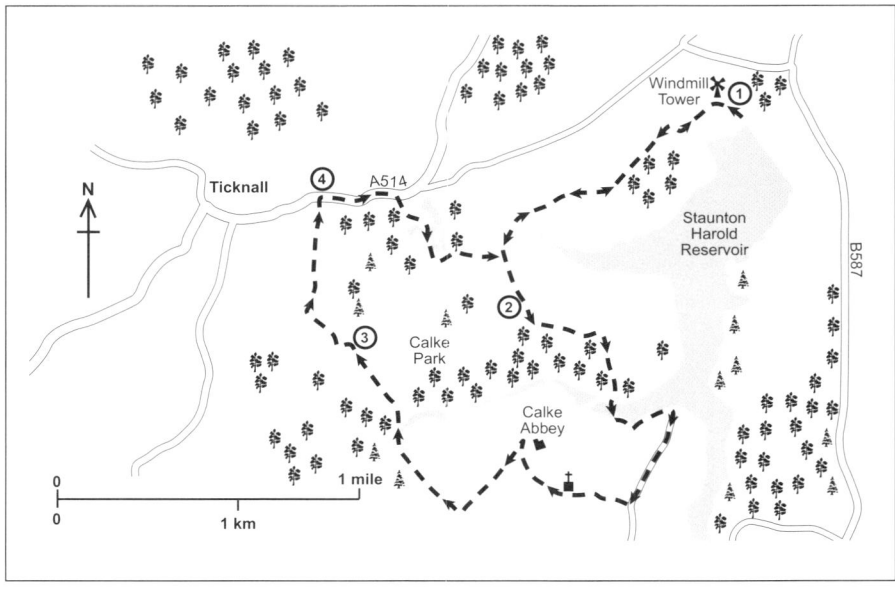

illustrate a house that has changed little since the 1880s and the Trust has deliberately decided to preserve it like that as a way of reflecting the social changes of the 20th century that led either to the demolition of many country houses or their conversion to other uses. Therefore do not expect elegance or grandeur. The house is old fashioned – electricity was not installed until as late as 1962 – shabby and full of clutter but, at the same time, different and interesting.

Calke Abbey

There was probably a medieval priory on the site and later an Elizabethan mansion but the present house was built by Sir John Harpur between 1701 and 1704. Some of the Harpurs were renowned for their eccentricity, in particular an obsession with natural history, and the house reflects this, containing an enormous collection of hunting trophies, stuffed animals and other curiosities, plus many works of art and a variety of tools and implements. All in all it is estimated that there are over 10,000 items. There is also an unusual 18th century bed. The superb restored orangery and fine walled gardens are well worth a visit and the magnificent parkland, over 600 acres in area, is renowned for its ancient oaks, pastures, deer enclosure and pools.

Calke Park

In the nearby church, built in 1826, there is a monument to Sir John Harpur and his wife.

Continue along the drive to the outbuildings of the house. These include the stable block, tearoom and an information centre where you purchase tickets to visit the house, gardens and church. The walk continues to the left along a drive across open parkland. In front of a gate, follow the drive to the right, pass the end of Mere Pond, go through a gate and continue along the drive to a lodge.

3. After going under an arch by the lodge, turn left alongside a fence bordering woodland as far as a well-surfaced track and turn right along it. Keep along this winding track, climb a stile and continue, later keeping along the right edge of a field. The houses and church at Ticknall can be seen over to the left. Climb a stile in the field corner, continue along the right edge of the next field and climb a stile onto a road.

To the left is the attractive and now quiet estate village of Ticknall, once a busy hive of industry with limestone quarrying and brick making activities. Its church dates from 1842 but fragments of its medieval predecessor survive in the churchyard.

Looking towards Ticknall church

4. The route continues to the right, passing under an arch. This is the Tramway Bridge, built in 1802 to carry a tramway that ran from the quarries and brickworks of Ticknall to the Ashby Canal at Willesley. Continue along the road for ¼ mile (400m) and at a public footpath sign, turn right along a tarmac track. The track curves left and right and passes beside a barrier to enter woodland. It later bends left and at a fork, keep ahead along the right hand narrower path, heading gently uphill to a stile. Climb it, keep ahead along the right edge of a field but after a few yards – just after passing a lone tree on the left, turn left onto a clear straight path which heads gently downhill across the middle of the field. This is where you rejoin the outward route and retrace your steps to the start.

WALK 7
A Rural Walk in a Town Centre:
Burton upon Trent

For a short walk in the middle of a busy town this one is hard to beat. The views across the Washlands, the flood plain of the River Trent, are superb and both the flower beds at Stapenhill Gardens and the tree-lined riverside paths are exceptionally attractive. A brief foray into the town centre of Burton to St Modwen's church and the Market Place provides a contrast with the rest of the walk.

Distance	2½ miles (4 km)
Approx. time	1½ hours
Starting point	Burton upon Trent, Stapenhill Road car park, grid ref SK255224
Parking	Stapenhill Road car park off the A444 on the east side of the River Trent. There are plenty of other car parks close to the walk which could be used, especially the Meadowside car park on the west side of the river just to the south of Burton Bridge
Terrain	Easy and flat walking mostly on tarmac riverside paths
Refreshments	Plenty of pubs and cafes at Burton upon Trent
Public transport	Buses from Uttoxeter, Swadlincote, Ashby-de-la-Zouch, Leicester, Lichfield and Derby; trains from Birmingham and Derby
Map	OS Explorer 245 (The National Forest)

The Walk

1. Start by heading down to the river and turn right, later curving right away from the Trent to a T-junction. Turn left to rejoin the riverbank and the

path ascends to emerge onto a road. Turn left and at a crossroads, turn left again to cross Burton Bridge – over ¼ mile (400m) wide – enjoying the views up and down the river.

There has been a bridge over the Trent here since the 12th century. The present structure was opened in 1864 and widened in 1926.

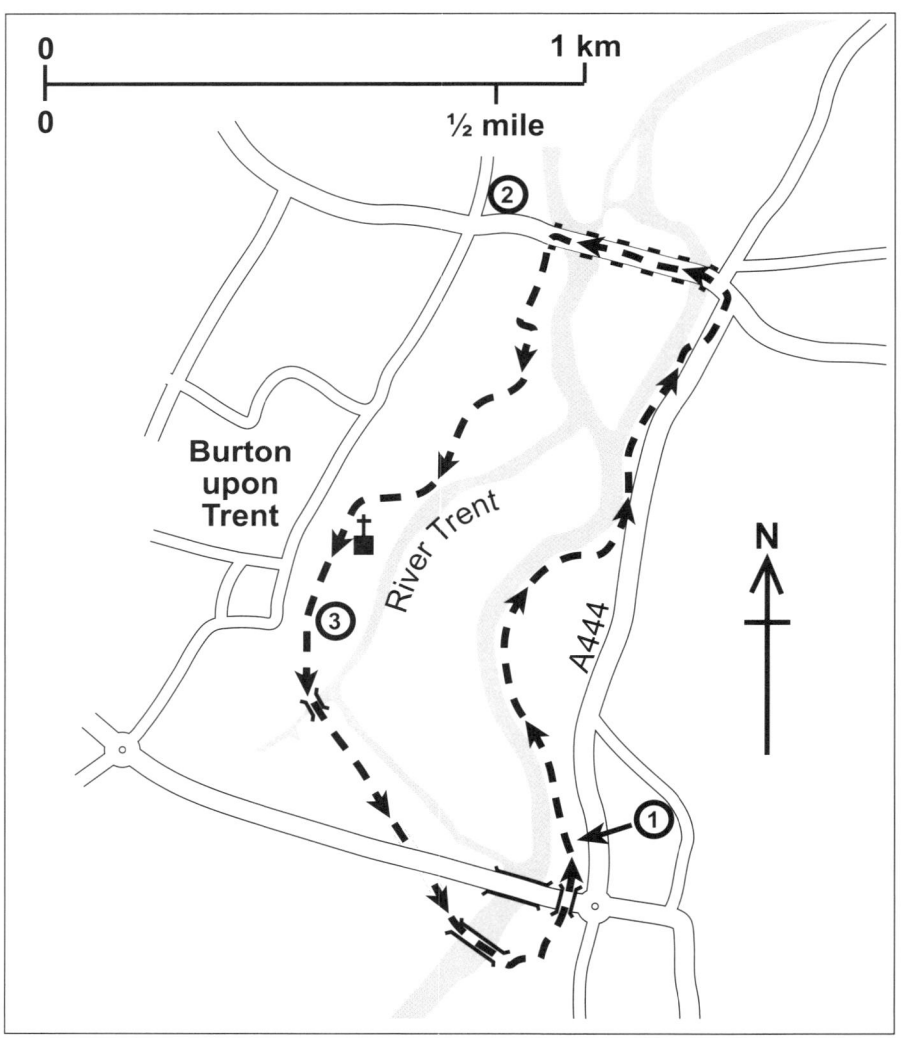

For centuries Burton has been a major centre of the brewing industry. The origins of this lie in the quality of the local water which contains minerals based on the presence of gypsum in the surrounding hills. This was discovered by monks from the now vanished medieval abbey who obtained the water from wells on the Trent Washlands. During its Victorian heyday around ¼ of all the beer in the country was brewed in Burton and there were over 30 breweries in the town. Nowadays the number of breweries has vastly declined but the town still remains an important brewing centre and there are several museums to the industry.

The tall brick tower that has dominated the skyline for much of the walk so far is connected with the brewing industry. It is the Bass Tower, a 120-foot (37m) high water tower built in 1866.

2. On the other side of the bridge turn left onto a tarmac track, initially walled. The winding track passes to the left of the Meadowside Leisure Centre, with its adjacent car park, and the library before curving right beside St Modwen's church into the Market Place.

The whole of the area around St Modwen's church and the Market Place occupies the site of the great medieval abbey of Burton, of which there are virtually no surviving remains. The church is Georgian, built around 1720, and the Market Hall was erected in the Victorian era.

St Modwen's church

At a footpath sign to Memorial Gardens and Technical College, turn left, passing in front of the Market Hall and Burton College. Keeping to the left side of the square, go under a bridge and continue between college buildings to a Washlands footpath post.

3. Turn left, in the Stapenhill Gardens direction, onto Stapenhill Viaduct. This raised footpath and cycleway takes you above the Washlands, under a road bridge and over the Ferry Bridge to the other side of the river.

The Trent Washlands, the flood plain of the river, comprise an attractive mixture of wetlands, meadows and woodlands and provide an unexpected leisure, recreation and wildlife amenity in the heart of the town. The river divides into several channels here, creating islands which can be accessed by bridges. The meadows are still used for grazing and have a surprisingly rural feel. It was the grazing of sheep and the collecting of water from the wells on these rich pastures by the medieval monks that created the two industries, wool and brewing, which became the bases of the prosperity of both the abbey and town of Burton.

Ferry Bridge replaced an earlier ferry and was opened in 1889. Stapenhill Viaduct was built at the same time and both were donated to the town by Lord Burton.

River Trent and the Trent Washlands at Burton

On the other side turn left into Jerrams Lane and immediately left again through Stapenhill Gardens and onto a riverside path. The path passes under St Peter's Bridge and continues by the river to the start.

WALK 8
A Fine Victorian Gothic Church:
Jackson's Bank and Hoar Cross

The walk starts and finishes in attractive woodland and the remainder of the route is across fields and along quiet lanes, passing the impressive Victorian church at Hoar Cross. There are fine views over Needwood Forest and the surrounding countryside.

Distance	4½ miles (7.2 km)
Approx. time	2 hours
Starting point	Jackson's Bank, grid ref SK140233
Parking	Jackson's Bank car park, on side road to Hoar Cross about ½ mile (0.8 km) west of Newchurch
Terrain	Woodland tracks and paths at the start and finish, lane and field paths in between, some modest climbs
Refreshments	None
Public transport	None
Map	OS Explorer 245 (The National Forest)

The Walk

The wooded ridge of Jackson's Bank forms part of the Needwood Estate owned by the Duchy of Lancaster. Much of it was replanted after widespread felling during World War II.
Just north of the car park is a 'Noon Column', one of six designed by the world renowned artist David Nash. Each of the 3-4 metre high columns is carved from sustainable English oak: they are placed so that, at noon each day, the sun shines through a slot carved in the wood, creating a line of light within the shadow cast by the column itself.

1. Turn left out of the car park along the road and at a public footpath sign, turn right beside a gate and walk along the right edge of a field. In the field corner keep ahead along a path through woodland, heading downhill and bending right. At the bottom turn right along a track to a lane. Turn left, cross a footbridge beside a ford and turn right at a T-junction.

2. At a public footpath sign, turn left through a kissing gate, go up steps, on through another gate and keep ahead by a fence bordering farm buildings on the left. Continue to a kissing gate, go through and walk along the the right edge of a field. Follow the field edge to the left and continue up to a stile in the corner. Climb it, bear left and head diagonally across the field in the direction of the tower of Hoar Cross church. Climb a stile, turn left and follow the field edge as it bends left and right to a hedge corner. Turn left, climb a stile onto a road and turn right to Hoar Cross church.

This imposing sandstone church was built in the 1870s by Emily Meynell-Ingram, of the adjacent Hoar Cross Hall, as a memorial to her husband

Hoar Cross church

48

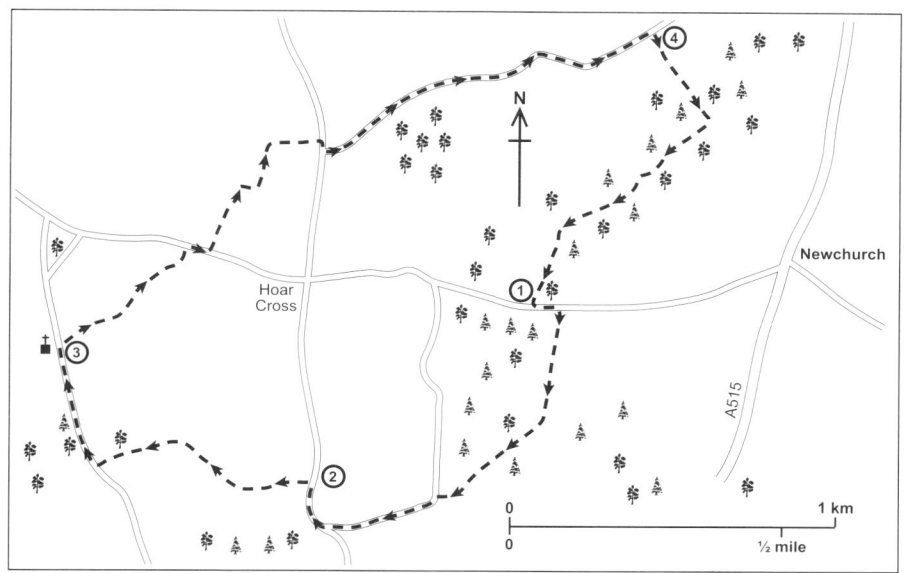

who was killed in a hunting accident. It was designed by G.F. Bodley, one of the foremost architects of the time, and is regarded as one of the finest Victorian Gothic churches in the country.

3. Opposite the church, turn right through a kissing gate and walk across a small wooded area to a stile. From here there is a superb view over the well-wooded landscape of Needwood Forest. After climbing the stile, bear slightly left downhill into a dip and continue across the field, looking out for a stile in the hedge on the right. Climb it, walk down three steps and turn left along a left field edge. After about 50 yards (46m), bear right across the field and look out for a stile in the fence in front. Climb it, keep ahead along an enclosed path and climb another stile onto a road. Turn right and at a public footpath sign, turn left over a stile and walk across the field

View over Needwood Forest

towards a solitary tree. Continue past it to the next tree, bear slightly left and follow the old tree line to a stile and footbridge in the right hand field corner just in front of electricity cables. Turn right over the stile, cross the plank footbridge, walk along the right field edge and climb a stile onto a road. Turn right, almost immediately turn left along a pleasant, quiet, shady lane and keep along it for about ¾ mile (1.2 km).

4. Shortly after passing a lane on the left, turn right through a kissing gate, cross a footbridge and walk along the right edge of a field. Go through a kissing gate in the corner, continue along an uphill path through woodland and at a crossways, turn right onto a track. Follow this winding and undulating track through the forest, keeping on the main track all the while and ignoring all side paths, to return to the start.

Woodland view from the car park

WALK 9
Villages, Woodlands and Canal:
Barton-under-Needwood

There is plenty of interest and a series of fine views on this varied walk in Needwood Forest. The first leg is an undulating route across fields, by both new and old woodlands and through two quiet and remote villages. Then comes a grand ridge walk with outstanding views across the Trent valley, followed by a stroll through woodland and by pools through part of Branston Water Park, to reach the towpath of the Trent and Mersey Canal. The final stretch is beside the canal, ending with a walk through a marina on the edge of Barton.

Distance	8 miles (12.9 km)
Approx. time	4 hours
Starting point	Barton-under-Needwood, by the war memorial in the village centre, grid ref SK188185
Parking	Barton-under-Needwood
Terrain	Fields, woodland, a few gentle gradients and a lengthy stretch along a canal towpath
Refreshments	Pubs and cafe at Barton-under-Needwood, pub at Tatenhill, pub at Barton Turn
Public transport	Buses from Lichfield and Burton upon Trent
Map	OS Explorer 245 (The National Forest)

The Walk

There are a number of attractive old buildings and several pubs in Barton-under-Needwood. As the name indicates, the village lies below the wooded slopes of Needwood Forest between the fringes of the old forest and the River Trent. The church was built in the early 16th century on the site of an earlier chapel, a rare example of a church built in the Tudor period.

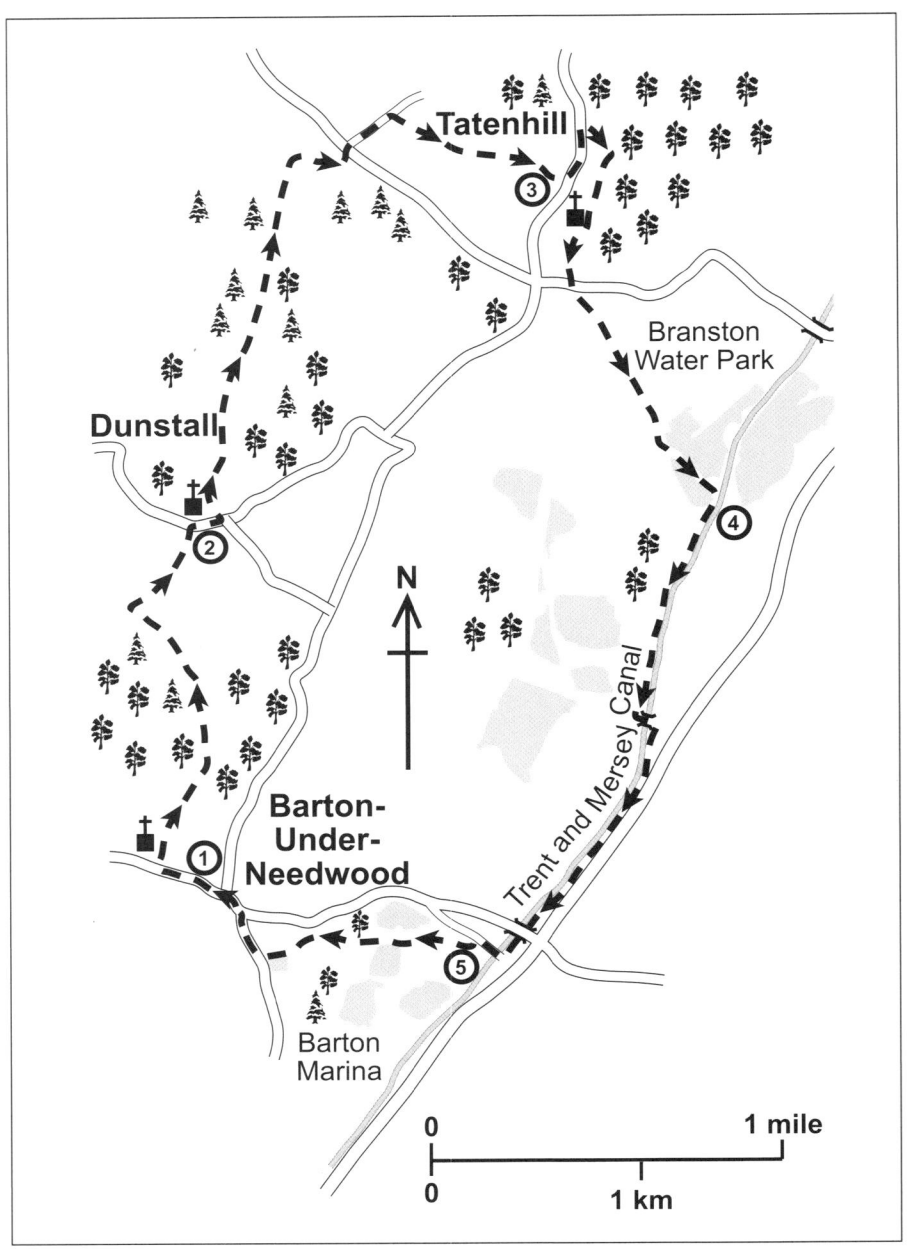

1. The walk starts in front of the war memorial. Facing the Shoulder of Mutton, turn left, passing to the right of the church, and after ¼ mile (400m), turn right, at a public bridleway sign, along a track to a gate. Go through, walk along a straight, enclosed track and where the track bends left, keep ahead to go through another gate. Follow a worn path across a field to a junction of paths and a footpath post, take the path to the left and continue across the field to a gate. Go through, here entering the woodland of Smith Hills, a mixture of recent plantings and mature trees, and continue through it, going through two more gates. After leaving the trees, continue in the same direction across a field, passing under electricity cables and making for a gate in the bottom left hand corner. To the right is an attractive view of Dunstall church. Go through the gate onto a track, turn right, go through another gate next to a cattle grid and continue along a tree-lined drive to emerge onto a road in front of the church.

Church at Barton-under-Needwood

Dunstall church

The tranquil hamlet of Dunstall comprises little more than the church, hall and a few farms and cottages. The church is Victorian, built in 1853.

2. Turn right and at a public bridleway sign, turn left gently uphill along a tarmac track. Where the track bends left to a farm, go through a gate and continue along an enclosed grassy track. Climb a stile, keep ahead, go

through a gate and continue straight across the next field to a gate on the far side. After going through it, walk along a wide, fence-lined track towards farm buildings, continue between barns and keep ahead along a tarmac track. Follow the track around a right bend but where it bends left, keep ahead through a gate, at a public footpath sign, and continue along an enclosed track. Bend left beside a house, go through a gate and keep ahead to a road. Turn left and almost immediately turn right along Cuckoo Cage Lane. At a public bridleway sign, turn right along a hedge-lined track, go through a gate and continue along a narrower enclosed path to go through another gate. Head diagonally across a field, go through a gate and keep along the left edge of the next field to a gate in the corner. Go through and continue downhill along the right field edge towards Tatenhill church, later veering left and heading down to go through a gate onto a road.

Tatanhill church

Like Dunstall, Tatenhill is a small village with a remote feel, though it does boast a pub. The church was once the major church in the area and mostly dates from the 13th century. It was restored in the 1890s.

3. Detour right if you wish to visit the church and – a little further on – the pub, but the route continues to the left through the village. At a public footpath sign, turn right along the bottom right hand edge of a field, follow the edge as it curves left and turn right through a kissing gate. Keep ahead below wooded slopes on the left, cross a path and turn left over a stile to enter Battlestead Hill Wood. The path bends right to head uphill through this beautiful wooded area. Keep ahead at a footpath post and at a fork a few yards ahead, turn right, in the direction of a National Forest Way sign. Turn left over a stile and head gently uphill, initially between mature woodland on the left and a new plantation on the right, continuing along a ridge. From here there are superb and extensive views across the Trent

View over the Trent valley from Battlestead Hill

valley. Keep along an undulating and well-waymarked path and after passing a bench, the path descends quite steeply, later by woodland on the left, to a T-junction.

Turn left, at a National Forest Way sign, go through a kissing gate and continue along an enclosed path to a road. Turn left and almost immediately at a National Forest Way sign, turn right along a wooded path which curves right to cross a footbridge over a brook. Go through a gate, turn left along a track, go through another gate and continue along an enclosed track. To the right is a low embankment bordering quarry workings. Where the track ends, go through a gate and continue along a narrower, winding tree-lined path along the left edge of one of the pools of Branston Water Park, eventually reaching the canal at Tatenhill Lock.

The Trent and Mersey Canal was opened in 1777 and linked the River Trent at Shardlow in Derbyshire with the River Mersey and Runcorn in Cheshire, a distance of 93 miles (149 km). Branston Water Park, a popular and attractive area of lakes, woodland and wetlands, has been created from a former gravel pit. There is a picnic area and visitor centre.

4. Turn right onto the towpath and at the first bridge (36), cross over to continue along the left side of the canal. Now comes a noisy stretch as the canal runs parallel to the busy A38. Continue under a succession of bridges as far as Bridge 38 where you bear left off the towpath.

Peaceful stretch of the Trent and Mersey Canal

5. Turn right to cross the bridge, walk along the road and turn left into Barton Marina. Turn right through the car park, take the well-surfaced path along the left side of a pool and at a fork, continue along the left hand path which curves right in front of another pool. Do not continue along this path but take the parallel grassy path, by a ditch on the right, go through a kissing gate and walk along an enclosed path, by a sports field on the left, and turn right over a footbridge and stile. Turn left along the left edge of a field and cross another footbridge and stile in the corner. Turn right along a track, climb a stile and continue by a tree-fringed pool on the left. Just before reaching a road, bear right across grass and go through a kissing gate onto the road. Turn right into Barton and at a T-junction, turn left along Main Street to the start.

WALK 10
A Waterside Ramble:
Fradley Junction and Alrewas

From the popular and bustling canal junction at Fradley, the first leg is an invigorating stroll along the towpath of the Trent and Mersey Canal to the village of Alrewas. This is followed by a walk across fields and along quiet lanes and enclosed tracks, with extensive views across the surrounding Staffordshire countryside.

Distance	5½ miles (8.9 km)
Approx. time	2½ hours
Starting point	Fradley Junction, by the cafe and information centre, signposted from the A513 to the west of Alrewas, grid ref SK142141
Parking	Fradley Junction
Terrain	Flat and easy walking on a canal towpath and along field paths
Refreshments	Pub and cafes at Fradley Junction, pubs at Alrewas
Public transport	None but you could start the walk at Alrewas which is served by buses from Lichfield, Tamworth and Burton upon Trent
Map	OS Explorer 245 (The National Forest)

The Walk

The canalside cottages and pub at Fradley Junction, the meeting place of the Coventry and Trent and Mersey canals, make an attractive scene. The Trent and Mersey Canal was opened in 1777 and linked the River Trent at Shardlow in Derbyshire with the River Mersey at Runcorn in Cheshire, a distance of 93 miles (149 km). The Coventry Canal, which runs between here and Coventry,

57

was completed in 1790. The original wharf buildings have been converted into a cafe, shop and information centre.

1. Facing the canal turn right alongside it, turn left over the first bridge and immediately turn right to continue along the other bank. Follow the towpath for just over 1½ miles (2.4 km) into Alrewas and in front of Bridge 48, leave the canal and head up to the road.

Trent and Mersey Canal near Alrewas

2. Cross over and continue along Mill End Lane, passing to the left of the church.

   The pleasant village of Alrewas gets its name from a combination of alder and marsh. Alder trees like damp conditions and thrived in the marshy low-lying ground by the Trent. It has a number of attractive old buildings, including some half-timbered, thatched cottages. The impressive sandstone church dates mainly from the 13th and 14th centuries but retains an earlier Norman doorway at the base of the tower.

Alrewas church

   Keep ahead at a junction – still along Mill End Lane – and where the lane ends, turn left, at a public footpath sign, along an enclosed path to a stile. Climb it, keep ahead along the left edge of a field, go through a kissing gate

Attractive track near Alrewas

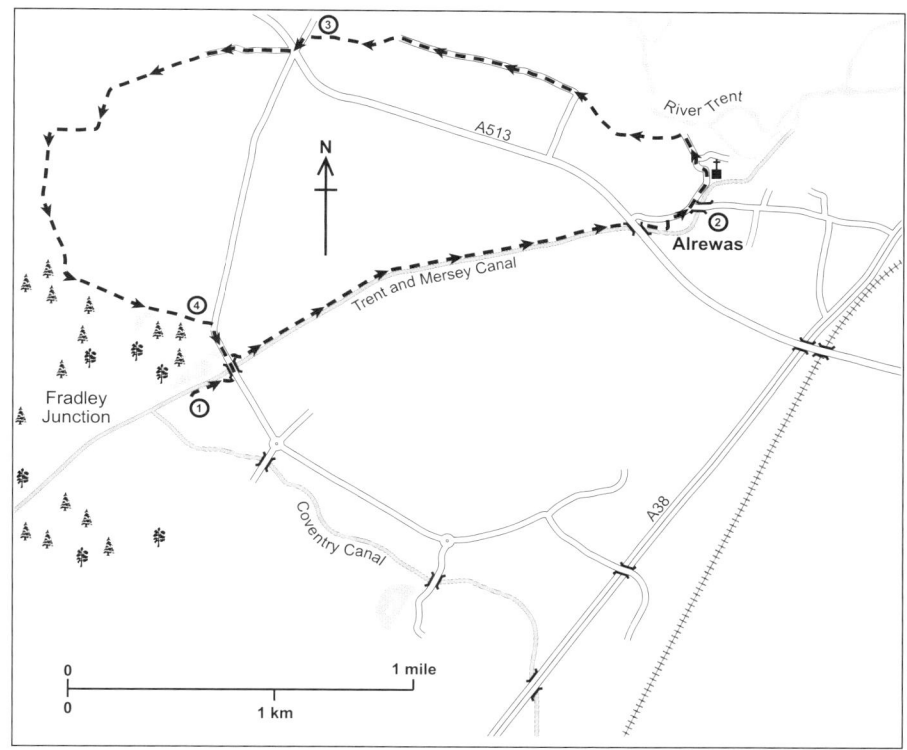

and continue along the right edge of the next field. In the corner turn right through a hedge gap and bear left to walk along a pleasant, hedge-lined track which emerges onto the corner of a narrow lane. Keep ahead along the lane and where it ends by Alrewas Gas Compressor Station, bear slightly left and continue along an enclosed tarmac track, by a high wire fence on the left. Follow the track across the middle of a field to the corner of a tarmac drive and keep ahead – Orgreave Hall can be seen to the right – along the tree-lined drive. Go through a gate to a crossways by a public footpath sign and turn left to the A513.

3. Cross over and bear right along a lane (Lupin Lane) which continues as a rough track along the right edge of a field. Go through a gate in the field corner and turn left along the left edge of two fields, going through a gate. In the corner of the second field, turn right to continue along its left edge and about halfway along, turn left through a gate. Walk along the right

59

field edge, continue along the right edge of a narrow belt of trees and keep along the right edge of the next field towards buildings. After crossing a brook, the way continues along a tarmac drive, keeping to the right of the buildings, and at a junction of tracks, bear left along another tarmac drive which curves left and continues beside a hedge on the right. Keep along this pleasant drive for ½ mile (800m) to emerge onto a road.

4. Turn right and after crossing the canal bridge, turn right again to return to the start.

Meeting of the Coventry and Trent and Mersey Canals at Fradley Junction

WALK 11
A Poignant Tribute:
National Memorial Arboretum, Alrewas and Wychnor

From the sylvan surroundings of the National Memorial Arboretum the route begins by taking you through the attractive village of Alrewas to the Trent and Mersey Canal. The canal towpath is followed to picturesque Wychnor church and on to Wychnor Lock. Soon afterwards you leave the canal, and lanes and tracks bring you to the banks of the River Trent near its confluence with the Tame. Here you re-enter the arboretum for a most attractive and leisurely final stretch through its grounds, much of it beside the River Tame, allowing plenty of time for a thorough exploration.

Distance	5 miles (8 km)
Approx. time	2½ hours
Starting point	National Memorial Arboretum, just off the A513 about ¾ mile (1.2 km) to the east of Alrewas, signposted from A513 and A38, grid ref SK181146
Parking	National Memorial Arboretum
Terrain	Some road walking but mostly along a canal towpath, tracks and and riverside paths
Refreshments	Cafe at the National Memorial Arboretum Visitor Centre, pubs at Alrewas
Public transport	None but you could start the walk from Alrewas which is served by buses from Tamworth, Lichfield and Burton upon Trent
Map	OS Explorer 245 (The National Forest)

The Walk

Conceived as a result of a visit to Washington in 1988, the National Memorial Arboretum is a most poignant and thought provoking place. It is managed by the Royal British Legion as a permanent monument to all who have suffered or died in the service of their country, not just in war but in their jobs or through acts of terrorism. Planting began in 1997 on land previously used for gravel extraction alongside the River Tame with funding provided by the National Forest Company. So far 40,000 trees have been planted but the project is evolving all the while and there is still much to do. There is a visitor centre with a shop and restaurant.

1. Begin by returning to the road and turn right, passing Alrewas Quarry, to the A38 on the edge of Alrewas. Turn right beside the road and, heeding the signs, turn left to cross this busy road very carefully and keep ahead along Main Street through the village. Just after passing the George and Dragon, turn right into Post Office Road and at a T-junction turn left to cross the canal bridge.

2. Immediately turn right, at a public footpath sign, onto the towpath of the Trent and Mersey Canal.

The pleasant village of Alrewas gets its name from a combination of alder and marsh. Alder trees like damp conditions and thrived in the marshy,

Trent and Mersey Canal between Alrewas and Wychnor

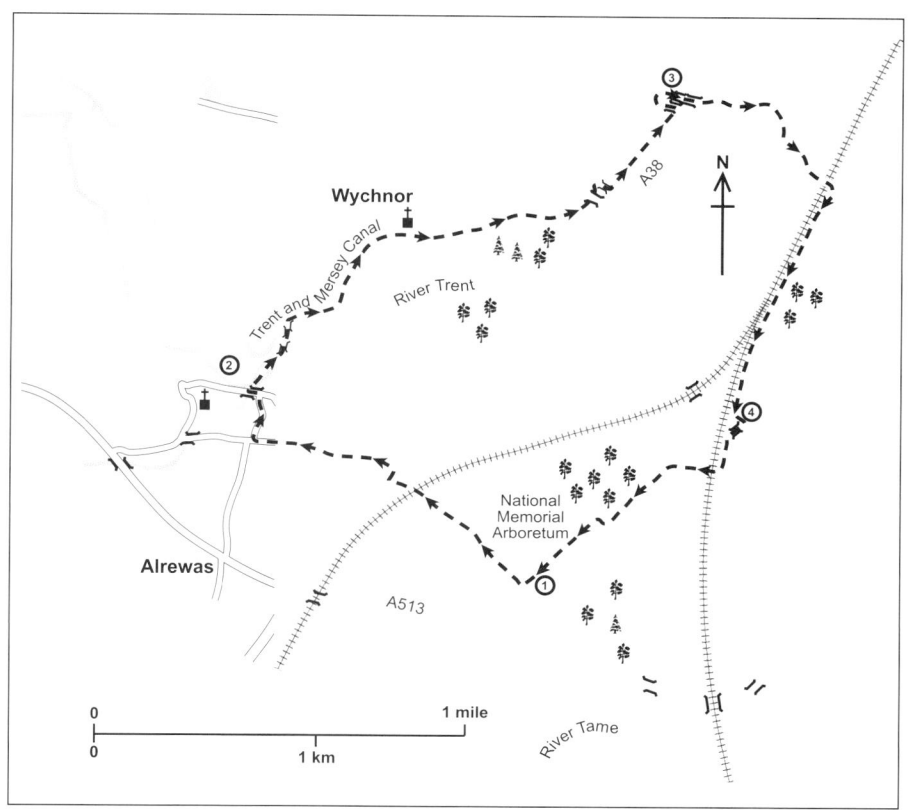

low-lying ground by the Trent. It has a number of attractive old buildings, including some half-timbered, thatched cottages. The impressive sandstone church dates mainly from the 13th and 14th centuries but retains an earlier Norman doorway at the base of the tower.

The Trent and Mersey Canal was opened in 1777 and linked the River Trent at Shardlow in Derbyshire with the River Mersey at Runcorn in Cheshire, a distance of 93 miles (149 km). Just beyond Alrewas the River Trent and canal briefly merge.

As you walk beside the canal a grand view opens up ahead of the tower of Wychnor church and you cross bridges over two arms of the River Trent where the river and canal merge. A little further on they separate again and the route continues by the canal. Just before a bridge a brief detour to the left over a stile, up across a field and through a kissing gate brings you to Wychnor church.

The medieval church at Wychnor has a delightful location just above the canal and overlooking the Trent valley. The village it once served, which declined during the Tudor period, had become virtually deserted by the 18th century and has all but disappeared. It is thought that the main reasons for this was the spread of enclosures and the migration of people to nearby industrial areas seeking work and higher wages. Its site is in the fields on the opposite side of the lane.

Return to the canal and follow it to Bridge 43 by Wychnor Lock. Turn right over the bridge, turn left to go under Bridge 42 and continue by the canal, which here runs parallel to the A38, as far as Bridge 41.

3. After passing under the bridge, turn right up the grass embankment, step over the crash barrier and turn right to cross the bridge. Keep along the road which curves right to a T-junction and turn right to cross a bridge over both the canal and A38. Where the road curves left, turn right onto another road – a sign indicates that this is a No Through Road – which curves left to a T-junction. Turn right along a track, passing Barton Quarry, and after crossing a railway bridge, turn right onto a broad, stony track parallel to the railway line. After ¾ mile (1.2 km) the track ends at a gate.

Wychnor church

4. Just before reaching this gate, bear right along a fence-lined path, turn right to cross Mythaholme footbridge over the

Confluence of the rivers Trent and Tame

River Trent and turn right again down another fence-lined path to a notice board welcoming you to the National Memorial Arboretum. Ahead are two paths; take the left hand one between woodland on the right and the river on the left to reach a picnic area which overlooks the confluence of the Trent and Tame. Turn right beside the River Tame and pass under a railway bridge to re-enter the National Memorial Arboretum.

Continue along a well-surfaced path beside the river, pausing to look at the various memorials passed on the right, as far as the Royal National Lifeboat Institution Memorial. At this point turn right away from the river and at a T-junction, turn left onto a broad straight path which leads back to the start.

Royal National Lifeboat Institution Memorial

The striking Armed Forces Memorial

WALK 12
A Forestry Transformation:
Rosliston and Coton in the Elms

The first and last parts of the route are through the attractive woodland adjacent to the Forestry Centre. After passing through the villages of Rosliston and Coton in the Elms, most of the remainder of the walk is across fields, with extensive views across the predominantly flat landscape to some of the woodlands planted through The National Forest scheme. Despite its proximity to busy main roads and the town of Burton upon Trent, this walk has a genuinely remote and tranquil feel.

Distance	3½ miles (5.6 km)
Approx. time	2 hours
Starting point	Rosliston Forestry Centre, ½ mile (800m) north of Rosliston village, grid ref SK244175
Parking	Rosliston Forestry Centre
Terrain	Flat walking mainly along field paths and woodland tracks
Refreshments	Cafe at Forestry Centre, pub at Rosliston, pub at Coton in the Elms
Public transport	Infrequent bus service from Swadlincote and Burton upon Trent
Map	OS Explorer 245 (The National Forest)

The Walk

Rosliston Forestry Centre is one of the flagship sites of The National Forest. Since 1993 grants from the National Forest Company, the Forestry Commission and South Derbyshire District Council have helped to transform a former farm just to the north of Rosliston village into the attractive recreational area whose wide ranging facilities include a visitor centre, shop, educational facilities and restaurant. There are walking trails, cycle tracks, children's play area, lakes, meadows and a mixture of old and more recent woodlands.

1. Start from the Visitor Centre entrance and turn left down a tarmac path into the car park. Turn left again, turn right in front of a bungalow and just before emerging onto the road, turn left along a track, signposted to Forest Lodges. Just before the track bends left, bear right onto a path, passing a public footpath sign, and follow it through attractive woodland. The houses and church spire at Rosliston soon come into view. At a public footpath sign to Rosliston, bear right through a fence gap and walk across a field. On the far side continue along an enclosed path, passing to the left of the churchyard, to a road in Rosliston village.

The small church at Rosliston was rebuilt in the early 19th century and the 14th century west tower is all that remains of its medieval predecessor.

Woodland near Rosliston

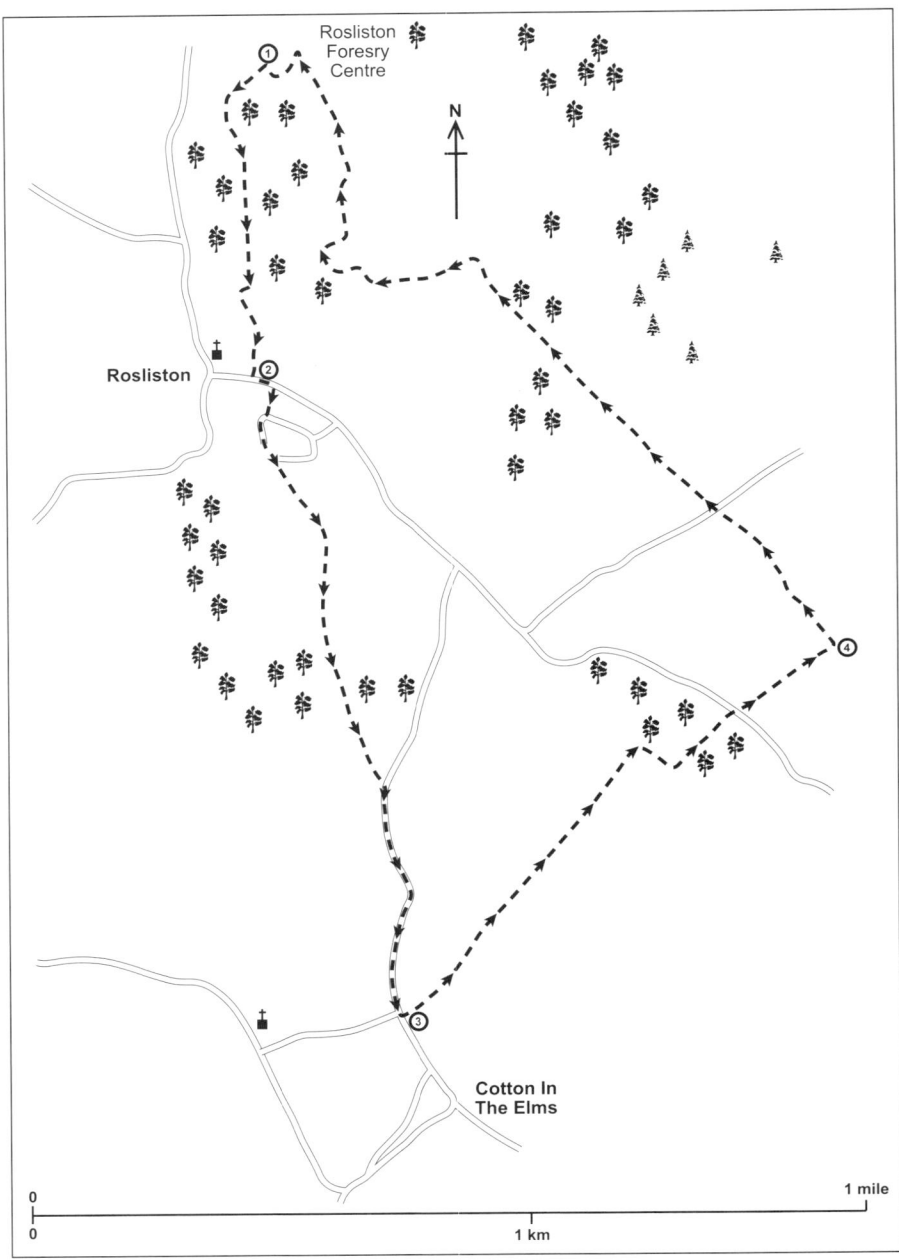

2   Turn left along the road and look out for an enclosed, fence-lined tarmac track on the right. Walk along it to a road in a modern housing estate, keep ahead along it and where it ends in front of two bungalows, bear left along a grassy enclosed path to a stile. Climb it, walk along a left field edge, continue along the curving left edge of the next field, climb a stile in the corner and keep ahead across a narrow grassy area towards farm buildings. Climb a stile, keep ahead, climb another one, passing to the left of the buildings, and continue along a hedge-and tree-lined track to a road. Turn right and follow the road to the edge of Coton in the Elms.

Keep ahead if you wish to explore the village. The elm trees that gave this former farming and mining village its name have long since gone, the victims of Dutch elm disease, but Coton is an attractive village with a triangular green watered by a stream and frequented by ducks. The Victorian church was built in 1846.

3. To continue the route, turn left, at a public footpath sign opposite Elms Road, along a tarmac track to a kissing gate. Go through and walk across

Pleasant landscape near Coton in the Elms

a field, keeping close to its right edge. Where the hedge on the right ends, veer slightly left and head across the rest of the field, making for a waymarked post on the far side next to a gate. Go through the gate – and another one immediately in front – and head straight across the next field to a hedge corner where there is a public footpath sign by a pool. Keep by the right field edge and climb a stile in the corner. Turn right along a narrow, enclosed path to emerge onto a track and keep ahead along the wider track.

4. At a notice 'Walkers This Way', turn left along a tree-lined, grassy track through woodland and climb a stile onto a lane. Turn right and after a few yards, look out for a public footpath sign in the hedge on the left. Squeeze through a gap in the hedge and take the straight path ahead across a large field. When you are close to two isolated trees on the left, turn left onto another straight path and continue across the field, passing to the left of the two trees. On the far side go through a hedge gap onto a road, cross over and continue along the track opposite to a gate. Go through, continue along the left edge of a field and pass through a hedge gap in the corner onto a track. Keep ahead and in front of a sign 'No Public Access', turn left onto a grassy path, later keeping by the left field edge. Follow the edge to the right and the path then bends left to a stile. Climb it to enter Rosliston Wood, bending right to emerge onto a well-surfaced track. Turn left to a footpath post at a path junction and turn sharp right onto another well-surfaced track. Keep along it – now on the National Forest Way – through woodland. At a crossways turn left, following directions to Centre, and a short, gentle climb leads back to the start.

WALK 13
The Forest's Industrial Heritage:
Moira Furnace and the Ashby Canal

This walk is in the heart of the National Forest and vividly illustrates the changes that have taken place recently in the landscape of what was once a busy, noisy and unattractive mining area. Coal tips and colliery buildings have been replaced by woodland, small lakes, nature reserves and picnic sites but the industrial heritage is preserved through the canal and the fascinating group of buildings around Moira Furnace. The walk utilises two means of transport once used to carry coal: the Ashby Canal and a disused railway track, the latter now the Ashby Woulds Heritage Trail.

Distance	4½ miles (7.2 km)
Approx. time	2½ hours
Starting point	Moira Furnace, just off B5003 to west of Moira village, grid ref SK114153
Parking	Moira Furnace, Crescent car park
Terrain	Easy flat walking on tracks, field paths and a canal towpath, with one stretch along a road
Refreshments	Tea room at Moira Furnace, pub at Donisthorpe
Public transport	Buses from Coalville, Ashby-de-la-Zouch, Burton upon Trent, Leicester and Swadlincote
Map	OS Explorer 245 (The National Forest)

The Walk

Moira gets its name from the Earls of Moira who owned much of the land in the locality and it was the 2nd earl who began the development of many of the coal mines around the village in the early 19th century. He also built the blast

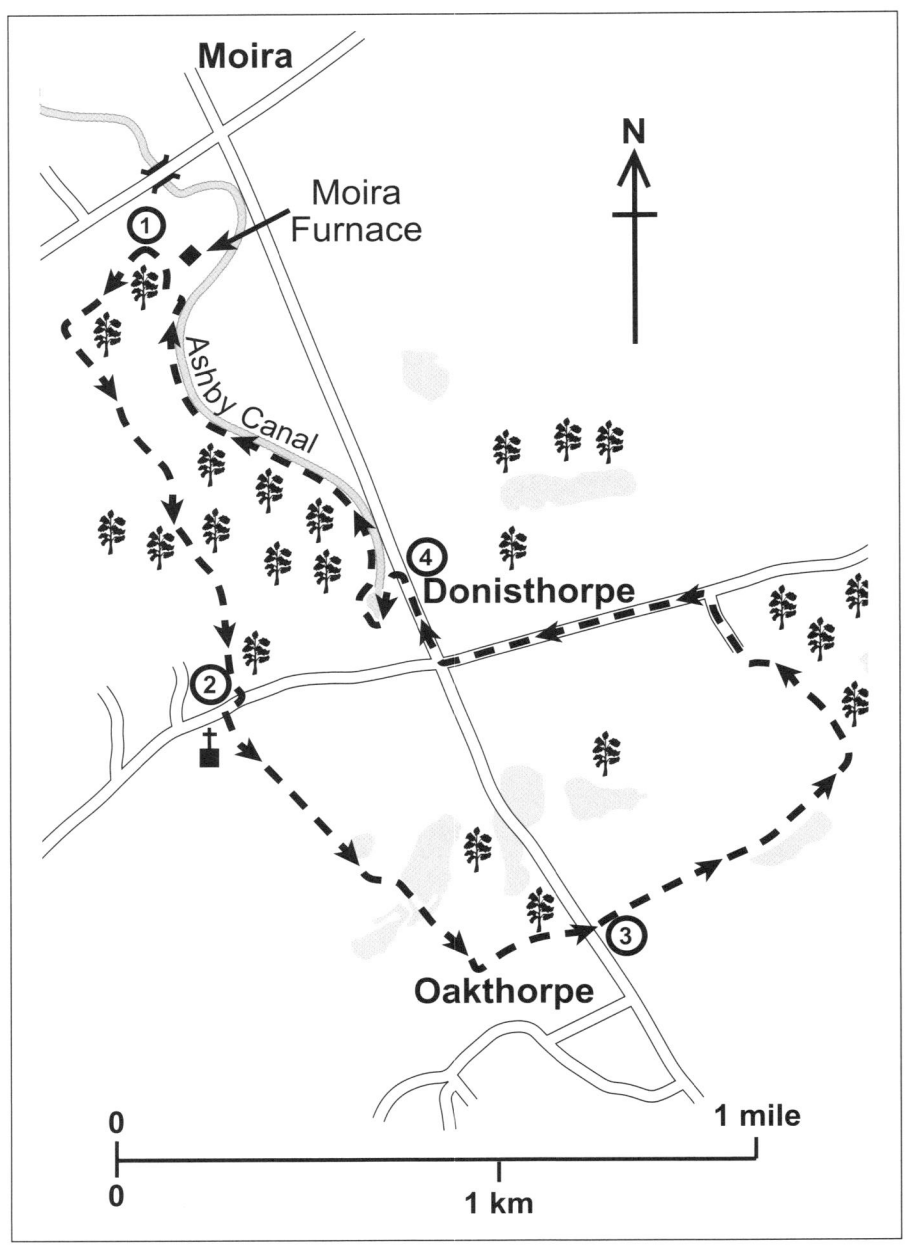

furnace beside the recently completed Ashby Canal in 1806 in order to process iron ore extracted from the coal deposits. It was never successful, mainly because of insufficient quantities of ore and considerable variation in its quality, and the furnace was closed the following year. An attempt was made to start it up again in 1810 but after only nine months it closed down for good.

Moira Furnace and the adjacent limekilns have been restored and opened to the public as a museum, with displays and information boards explaining how the furnaces worked. The site also has craft workshops and a small nature reserve.

1. Facing the children's play area, turn left across the car park and continue across a sports field, making for the far left hand corner. Cross the end of a tarmac track and continue along the path opposite which curves left into woodland. Just before reaching a kissing gate, turn right up a flight of steps to the top of a railway embankment and turn left onto a path.

The path is part of the Ashby Woulds Heritage Trail between Moira and Measham which runs along the former track of the Ashby and Nuneaton Joint Railway. The railway was opened in 1873 to carry coal from the local mines to London and the south of England. It finally closed in 1981.

The path soon passes through Donisthorpe Woodland Park.

Woodland near the start of the walk

The woodland park has been established on the site of the former Donisthorpe Colliery. Soon after its closure in 1990, the site was acquired from British Coal and most of the planting was carried out in 1996-97. Funding was provided by The National Forest Company and it is a superb example of how a former industrial area can be made attractive again and provide recreational facilities. A series of information boards illustrate the immense task involved in achieving this transformation in a relatively short time.

Follow the path, winding in places, over a stream and it eventually emerges onto a road.

2. Cross over, turn right and the path curves left into a parking area by Donisthorpe's early 19th century church. Turn left to continue along the disused railway track but at a fork take the left hand path, here leaving the Heritage Trail. Go through a fence gap and the enclosed path continues along the backs of houses to a stile. Climb it, walk along the right edge of a field and keep ahead through a belt of trees. After crossing a footbridge, there follows a most attractive part of the route as you continue between pools, over marshy land and then along a left field edge, with views of the village of Oakthorpe in front. An enclosed section rises gently to reach the end of a lane where you pass beside a metal gate. Turn left along a track, climb a stile and keep ahead along the left edge of a field. Climb another stile onto a road and turn right.

3. At a public footpath sign to Willesley Wood just beyond a 30 mph sign, turn left over a stile. Walk along a left field edge, climb a stile, descend steps and continue straight ahead across the next field, making for a waymarked post on the far side. Bear slightly right to walk along the left edge of a field and the path curves first left and then right, descends gently through trees and bushes and continues along the left edge of an attractive

Pool near Willesley Wood

pool. After climbing a stile, keep ahead to a crossways and turn left onto a path which heads through part of Willesley Wood which occupies the site of the former Oakworth Colliery. Later the path widens into a track and emerges onto a road. Turn left into Donisthorpe and at a crossroads turn right along Moira Road.

4. Just past the last of the houses on the left, turn left into Donisthorpe Woodland car park and head uphill and through a gate to the Ashby Canal. Turn left and then right across the end of the canal and turn right again along the towpath.

Ashby Canal

The Ashby Canal was built between 1794 and 1804 and linked the coal mines around Moira with the Coventry Canal at Marston Junction near Nuneaton. It declined after it was largely superseded by the railway and this, coupled with instability caused by mining subsidence, led to its closure in the 1940s. The short stretch from here to Conkers Discovery Centre has been restored and there are plans to open up more. The southerly, more agricultural section of the canal from Snarestone is still in use and is a popular recreational amenity.

Moira Furnace

Follow the canal to Moira Furnace and in front of the bridge, turn left downhill beside the furnace. Keep ahead along a tarmac drive and take the first turning on the left to return to the car park.

WALK 14
Ivanhoe's Castle:
Ashby-de-la-Zouch, Blackfordby and Smisby

The walk takes you across the gently rolling countryside to the west, north and east of Ashby-de-la-Zouch. Initially a straight path leads across fields to the hilltop village of Blackfordby. From here you head across to Smisby and a gentle descent brings you back to the town centre of Ashby. There are a number of fine and extensive views and the route passes by several recently planted woods created through The National Forest project.

Distance	7 miles (11.3 km)
Approx. time	3½ hours
Starting point	Ashby-de-la-Zouch, Market Square in front of the Town Hall and Market building, grid ref SK358167
Parking	Ashby-de-la-Zouch
Terrain	Mainly field and woodland paths and tracks with a few gentle gradients
Refreshments	Pubs and cafes at Ashby, pub at Blackfordby, pub at Smisby
Public transport	Buses from Leicester, Coalville, Burton upon Trent and Swadlincote
Map	Map: OS Explorer 245 (The National Forest)

The Walk

Although situated in the former Leicestershire coalfield with industrial towns and mining villages nearby, Ashby-de-la-Zouch never became industrialised itself and retains the atmosphere of a pleasant and traditional old market town. It gets its name from the Zouches who became lords of the manor in 1160 and added their family name to distinguish the town from other Ashbys in the Midlands.

In the 15th century the manor passed to the powerful Hastings family and Sir William Hastings was given royal permission to transform the fortified manor house into a strong castle. He mainly did this by constructing the impressive Hastings Tower, around 90 feet (27m) high and comprising four storeys. As a Royalist stronghold in the Civil War, Ashby Castle had to endure a lengthy siege by Parliamentary forces during which the Hastings Tower was split in two. After the war the castle was slighted on the orders of Cromwell's government but in the 19th century Sir Walter Scott caused a renewal of interest in it by making it the setting for his Ivanhoe stories.

The nearby church was built in the 15th century and restored and enlarged in 1880. Inside there are monuments to the Hastings family.

1. Facing the Town Hall and Market, turn right along Market Street and at a junction, keep ahead uphill along Kilwardby Street. The street continues as Moira Road and soon after going over the brow of a hill, turn right into Highfields Close. Turn left at a T-junction and where the road ends, turn right onto an enclosed tarmac path. The path bears left along the right edge of a sports field to a road. Cross over and the well-waymarked route continues in a more or less straight line across a series of fields, over stiles and through hedge gaps, heading gently uphill towards Blackfordby. Finally you climb a stile onto a lane which leads into the village.

The path between Ashby and Blackfordby

The tiny village of Blackfordby retains a few old thatched cottages. The church was originally a chapel which had fallen into disrepair by the Victorian era and was rebuilt in the 1850s.

2. Keep ahead to a T-junction in order to visit the pub and church but just before reaching there, the route continues to the right along an enclosed track. The track curves right between trees to a gate. Go through, bear left along the left field edge to a junction of paths by a waymarked post and

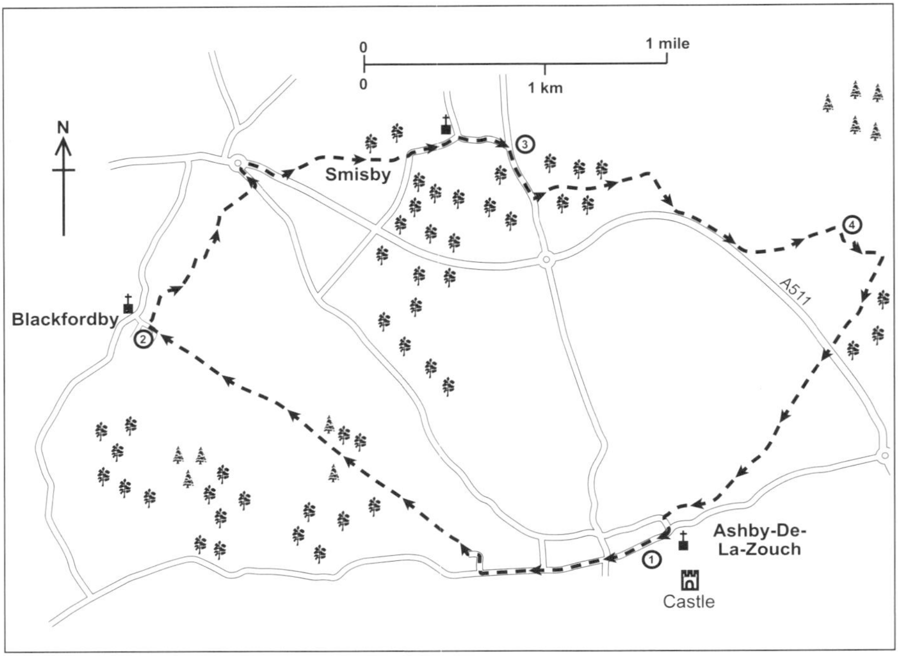

keep ahead, later bearing right to another waymarked post. Turn left through a fence gap, head across the field, go through another gap and continue across the next field, making for a stile on the far side.

After climbing it, cross the road, turn left up to a roundabout and turn sharp right beside the A511. Opposite a public footpath sign pointing to the right, carefully cross the busy road, turn right and almost immediately descend an embankment and go through a kissing gate. Walk across to a stile, climb it, keep ahead to climb another one and continue to a field corner where you cross a plank footbridge and climb a stile into the next field. Continue across it, climb a stile on the far side and walk along a narrow path between trees (this may be

Smisby church

overgrown in the summer). The path later widens into a track to reach a kissing gate. Go through and keep along a lane into the village of Smisby.

Smisby is a traditional farming village just across the Leicestershire-Derbyshire border. The fine church is mainly 14th century with a 15th century tower. It was restored in the late 19th century.

After passing the church, the lane bears slightly right and continues through the village to a T-junction.

3. Turn right and after ¼ mile (400m), turn left along a lane – there is a sign here Public Bridleway 150 yards ahead – passing between the National Forest woodlands of Woodcote. The lane becomes more of a tarmac drive and where it curves left to a farm, turn right beside a barrier, by a public bridleway sign, and walk along a track by a wire fence on the left. The track bears left and for a while keeps parallel to the A511. From here there are extensive views to both right and left. Follow the track to the gates of a farm

Ruins of Ashby Castle

79

4. Turn right along the left edge of a field to emerge onto a tarmac drive. Continue along it and at a junction of tracks and paths (just before the track curves left), turn right along a hedge-lined track, here joining the well-waymarked Ivanhoe Way. At a fork take the right hand track – now attractively tree-lined - pass under the A511 and keep ahead, passing by the huge McVitie's building, largely screened from the path by trees.

   Where the track bears slightly left, turn right over a plank footbridge and walk along an enclosed path. Look out for where you turn right over another footbridge, turn left and the path bends right to enter a field. Turn left, follow the path across the field towards the corner of houses and continue on to a kissing gate in the far corner. Go through, continue across the next field, go through a hedge gap, walk along the left field edge and go through another kissing gate. Take the enclosed path opposite which continues along a left field edge. It becomes enclosed again and finally a tarmac track brings you onto a road. Turn left and at a T-junction, turn right and walk down Market Street to return to the start.

WALK 15
Hall, Church and Parkland:
Staunton Harold

Much of the first half of the walk is across part of the well wooded Staunton Harold Estate, giving you the opportunity to see the unforgettable and highly photogenic combination of hall, church and lake situated amidst rolling parkland. The return leg is across fields with some fine and extensive views.

Distance	5½ miles (8.9 km)
Approx. time	3 hours
Starting point	Car park at southern end of Staunton Harold Reservoir, take lane signposted to Calke from B587, grid ref SK378220
Parking	Severn Trent car park
Terrain	Woodland, parkland and field walking, gentle terrain
Refreshments	Tea room at Ferrers Craft Centre at Staunton Harold Hall
Public transport	None
Map	OS Explorer 245 (The National Forest)

The Walk

1. From the car park take the path that heads down to the lane. Bend right to cross the end of the reservoir and shortly turn left to enter the Dimminsdale Nature Reserve, here joining the National Forest Way.

Staunton Harold Reservoir was constructed in 1964 and extends over an area of 209 acres. It has become an important wildlife habitat and a popular centre for water sports, fishing, bird watching, cycling and walking. The nature reserve has been created from a former limestone quarrying

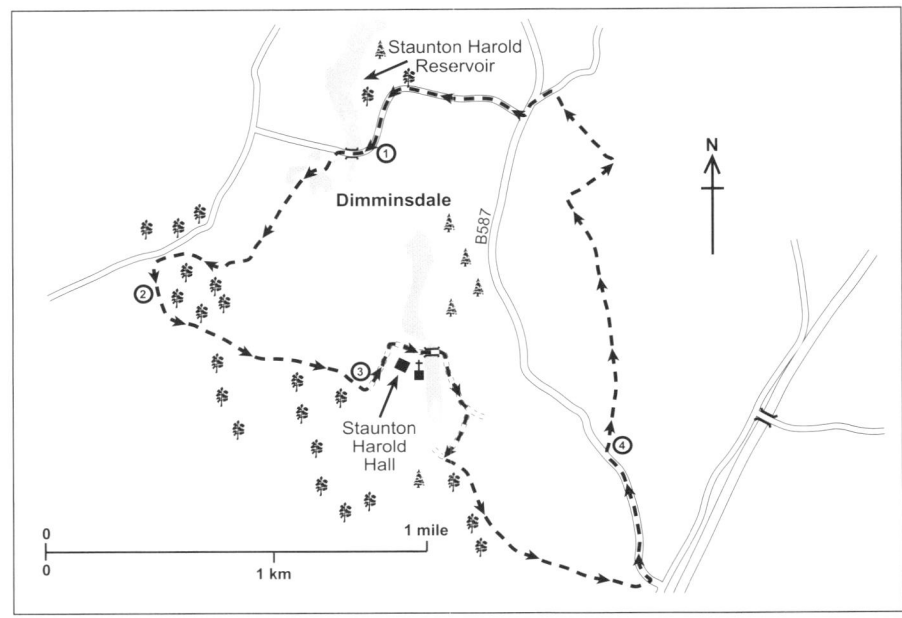

area worked since the Middle Ages and the numerous small pools were formed when the disused quarries filled up with water. In February it is noted for its superb display of snowdrops.

Follow a winding path through the wooded reserve and after descending steps to a T-junction, turn right onto a path which later bends sharply left to cross a footbridge over a stream. Climb steps and at a National Forest Way sign, turn right through a squeezer stile. Keep

Staunton Harold Reservoir from its southern end

along a path, go through a gate, here leaving the woodland, and continue along the left edge of a field, bearing left to emerge onto a lane. Turn right to a road junction, turn left and almost immediately turn left again through a gate, at a public footpath sign. Keep ahead to cross a plank footbridge, go through a gate, walk along an enclosed path and go through another gate onto a tarmac drive.

2. Turn left and look out for a public footpath sign on the left where you go through a kissing gate. Walk along the right field edge, go through a kissing gate, keep along the right edge of the next field and just before the corner, turn right through another kissing gate. Turn left along a left field edge, go through a gate and continue along the field edge towards woodland. After going through a kissing gate in the field corner, keep along the right edge of the next two fields, going through another kissing gate. In the corner of the last field (in front of a National Forest information board), turn left along a track, go through a gate and turn right along a tarmac drive.

3. Just before entering woodland, turn left onto a path that keeps along the right edge of a car park, cross a footbridge and continue through trees to the Ferrers Craft Centre. To the right is a view of Staunton Harold Hall and church but these views become more stunning during the next ¼ mile (400m). Keep ahead on joining a tarmac drive which curves right to a T-junction. Turn right to visit the church; otherwise turn left and cross a bridge over the lake.

In Dimminsdale Nature Reserve

The scene of the hall and church at Staunton Harold in close proximity, standing above the lake and surrounded by parkland, could hardly be more typically English. It is all the work of one family, the Shirleys, who owned the estate from 1423 to 1954. Despite this both the hall and family have had a very chequered history.

One member was sent to the Tower of London in the Cromwellian period but later in the 17th century the family fortunes revived and the title Earl Ferrers was given to the Shirleys by Queen Anne in 1711. In 1760 the 4th earl was hanged for killing his steward and the family was plagued by debts during the late 19th and early 20th centuries. In 1954 these debts led to the sale of the estate and the hall became first a Cheshire Home and later a Sue Rider Home. Since 2003 it has been owned by John Blunt. The present hall, a restrained and dignified Classical design, was built in the 18th century and the formal gardens were laid out at the same time.

The church was built by Sir Robert Shirley in 1653, a rare example of a church dating from the Cromwell era. Built in a traditional Gothic style, this bold Anglican gesture was really a sign of defiance to Oliver Cromwell and the Puritans, hence sir Robert's incarceration in the Tower of London. It was given to the National Trust prior to the sale of the estate in the 1950s.

Classic English scene of Staunton Harold Hall and church from across the lake

Continue through the ornamental gates and take the first track on the right. Go through a kissing gate by a cattle grid, pass beside a gate and turn right along a tarmac drive. Where the drive bends right, turn left through a gate along a gently ascending track. At a junction by a waymarked post, keep ahead and the track eventually bends left to a drive.

Turn right to a road, turn left, in Reservoir and Calke Abbey direction, and after ½ mile (800m) you reach a public footpath sign on the right. A layby on the opposite side of the road gives a fine view of the hall, church and lake nestling in the valley below.

4. At the footpath sign turn right through a hedge gap and head in a straight line across a field. From here there is a view of the hilltop church at Breedon, a prominent landmark for miles around. Climb a stile on the far side, keep ahead to climb another one, walk along the right edge of a field and climb a stile onto a track. Walk along the right edge of the next field, turn right over a footbridge, climb a stile and continue along a left field edge. Go through a hedge gap, keep along the left edge of the next field but after a few yards, turn left over a double stile. Head across the field to a waymarked post on the far side, climb two stiles in quick succession, continue across the next field and on by the left field edge to a kissing gate. Go through onto a lane and turn left to a T-junction. Turn left in the Ashby direction and take the first lane on the right, signposted to Calke, to return to the car park.

WALK 16
Medieval Ruins:
Grace Dieu Priory and Wood

This is a short but extremely attractive and interesting walk in the Charnwood Forest area, ideal for a warm summer afternoon as most of it is in shady woodland but equally fine at any season of the year. Historic interest is provided by the atmospheric ruins of Grace Dieu Priory, one of the few surviving and accessible monastic remains in Leicestershire. The route is well-signed and easy to follow.

Distance	2½ miles (4 km)
Approx. time	1½ hours
Starting point	Bulls Head, Thringstone, grid ref SK431181
Parking	Car park behind the Bulls Head at Thringstone
Terrain	Flat walking mainly along woodland tracks, with a final stretch along a road
Refreshments	Pubs at Thringstone
Public transport	Buses from Coalville and Loughborough
Map	OS Explorer 245 (The National Forest)

The Walk

1. From the corner of the car park take the path, signposted to the Grace Dieu Trail, which bends to the right alongside the right edge of woodland. The path then bends left into the trees and passes under a disused railway bridge to a track. Turn left along the well-surfaced track which is the Grace Dieu Trail and part of Cycle Route 52. At a junction of paths and tracks, turn left to go under a viaduct and just before emerging from the trees,

turn right through a gate, at a sign 'Footpath to Priory'. Walk along a track and after going through a gate, the priory ruins are seen just ahead.

While visiting the local area, William Wordsworth wrote of the 'ivied ruins of forlorn Grace Dieu' lying beneath 'yon eastern ridge, the craggy bound, rugged and high, of Charnwood's forest ground'. Grace Dieu Priory was a small and rather poor Augustinian nunnery founded in the 13th century. After its dissolution by Henry VIII in the 1530s, it was converted into a residence by the new landowners and therefore the present scanty

Grace Dieu Wood

Remains of Grace Dieu Priory

remains are a rather jumbled mixture of medieval priory and Tudor house. After years of neglect and inaccessibility, the priory ruins have been recently restored and made the focal point of a nature trail.

2. Retrace your steps to where you first joined the Grace Dieu Trail by the disused railway bridge and continue along the track through Grace Dieu Wood.

Grace Dieu Wood is an ancient woodland, mainly comprising oak, holly and silver birch, recently enlarged through the National Forest scheme. The wood lies on the edge of Charnwood Forest and, together with Cademan and other neighbouring woods, it makes up some of the finest and most beautiful areas of broadleaved woodland in Leicestershire.

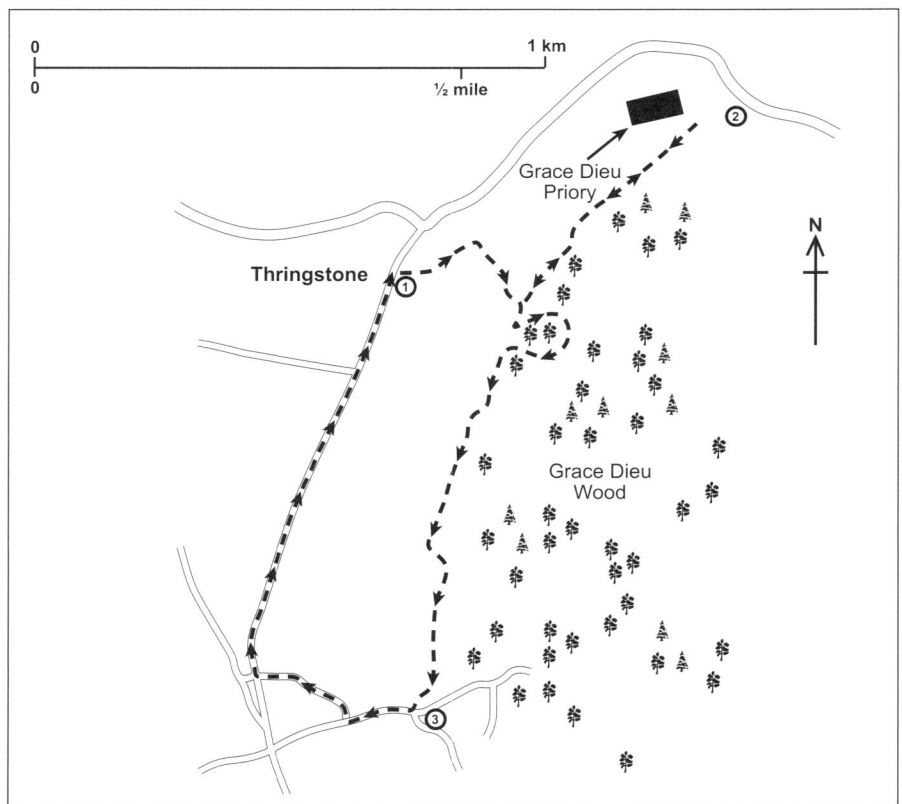

At a footpath sign for Grace Dieu Wood, turn left for a brief circuit of part of this beautiful woodland. At a fork in front of a National Forest notice, take the left hand path, turn right at a T-junction and at the next junction, follow the path to the right again. Turn left, here rejoining the Grace Dieu Trail and follow the track, still mainly through woodland, to a road.

3. Turn right and at a public footpath sign, turn right again onto a short stretch of path called Brook Lane. The brook is below on the right. Bear left to continue along a road which emerges onto the main road in Thringstone. Turn right along Loughborough Road and follow it back to the start, a distance of approximately ¾ mile (1.2 km).

WALK 17
From Opencast Mine to Forest Park:
Sence Valley

In such pleasant and quiet surroundings it is hard to believe that much of this route is across countryside only recently reclaimed from industry and mining. There is much historic interest, notably the medieval manor house at Donington le Heath and the ancient churches at Snibston, Ravenstone and Normanton le Heath. There is also clear visual evidence of the continuing development and evolution of the National Forest.

Distance	7½ miles (12.1 km)
Approx. time	4 hours
Starting point	Sence Valley Forest Park, off A447 ½ mile (0.8 km) north of Ibstock, grid ref SK404113
Parking	Sence Valley Forest Park
Terrain	Lanes, field paths and tracks, woodland areas and just a few gentle gradients
Refreshments	Pub at Donington le Heath, cafe at Donington le Heath Manor House, pub at Ravenstone
Public transport	Buses from Coalville and Hinckley
Map	OS Explorer 345 (The National Forest)

The Walk

Between 1982 and 1996 Sence Valley Forest Park was a vast opencast mining site. Since the end of mining operations, the planting of nearly 100,000 trees by the Forestry Commission has completely transformed the landscape and created an attractive recreational environment. The park was opened in 1998 and comprises 100 acres of woodland, lakes and grassland with fine views.

1. Start by walking back towards the road, not on the drive but along the parallel path to the left of it. The path turns left through a fence gap and later through a kissing gate to a track. Turn right, cross the A447 and, at a public footpath sign, keep ahead along a path across fields. At a footpath post, bear left across a field to another post and go through a hedge gap. Descend into a dip, climb gently out of it and continue diagonally across the large field to the far left hand corner.

   Bear right through a hedge gap, continue along the left edge of a succession of fields, going through a series of hedge gaps, and finally climb a stile onto a road. Turn left, pass between the supports of a former railway bridge and follow the road into Donington le Heath. Turn left beside the Corner Pin pub and head gently uphill through the village to the manor house.

The manor house at Donington le Heath is a late 13th century stone-built house, modernised and renovated in the 17th century. During its long history it has been owned by many families. One of the most illustrious of these was the Digbys who lost the house and surrounding lands in the Wars of the Roses but subsequently regained them, probably because Sir John Digby backed the right horse by fighting on the side of Henry Tudor at the battle of Bosworth in 1485. A later member of the family, Everard Digby, brother of the owner of Donington, was one of a number of people executed in 1605 for being involved in the Gunpowder Plot.

By the late 17th century the manor house had come into the possession of the Harleys who set up a trust. For the next 300 years it was rented out and used for a variety of purposes, including a pigsty. By the 1960s it was in a very bad state but in 1965 it was bought by Leicestershire County Council and subsequently restored as a period house. The 17th century gardens were restored at the same time. The house possesses a fine collection of 17th century furniture.

Medieval manor house at Donington le Heath

2. Where the road bends right by the manor house, turn left along Berry Hill Lane and at a public footpath sign, turn right along a left field edge. Climb

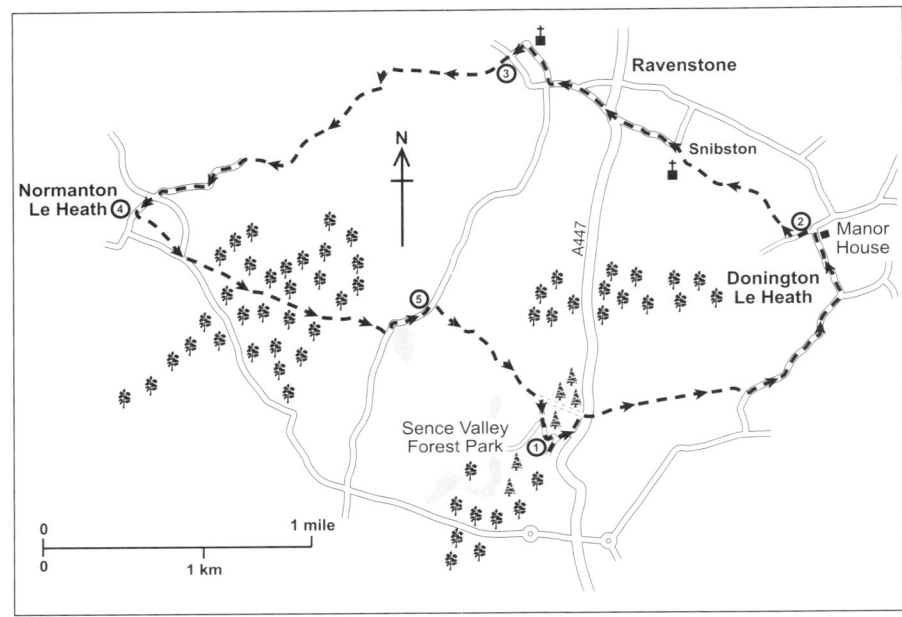

a stile, turn left to cut across the corner of the next field, making for a yellow-topped post, and continue along its left edge to a stile. Climb it, walk along the right field edge, go through a gate and continue along an enclosed track. The track passes between farm buildings and continues gently uphill to emerge onto the corner of a lane to the right of Snibston church.

Norman church at Snibston

The tiny 12th century church at Snibston stands in rural isolation away from the mining communities that grew up around Coalville during the Industrial Revolution. It is one of the smallest churches in the country.

Keep ahead along the lane to a main road on the edge of Ravenstone. Cross over, take the road ahead, signposted to Ravenstone Village Centre, and

The way across the fields near Ravenstone

bear left on joining another road. At a crossroads just beyond a pub, turn right along Main Street to the church and turn left into Hospital Lane.

The red sandstone Ravenstone church dates mainly from the 14th century. Nearby in Hospital Lane there are some attractive, brick-built almshouses.

3. At a T-junction cross the road, climb a stile opposite and walk along an enclosed path. After climbing the next stile, continue across a field, climb another stile and turn right to keep along a right field edge. Climb a stile in the corner and walk along the left edge of the next field towards woodland. A notice on the edge of the wood indicates that much of the land between here and Normanton, an area of 460 acres, is to be developed over the next few years as part of the Queen Elizabeth Diamond Jubilee Woods, a nationwide project to create 60 new woods to mark the 60 years of the Queen's reign. This is one of the major schemes, involving the creation of a lake and wetlands and the planting of over 300,000 native trees in the heart of the National Forest.

Turn right through a hedge gap into the wood and turn left onto a track that runs along the right inside edge of the trees. At a public bridleway sign, turn left to continue along another track, initially along the right inside edge of the wood. The track later becomes a hedge-lined, winding track but you need to look out for a sharp right bend – there is a kissing gate and another notice about the Jubilee Wood to the left here. The track eventually emerges onto a lane. Turn left into Normanton le Heath, cross a road and continue along the lane opposite to the church.

Although the M1, busy main roads and built up areas are not far away, there is a genuinely remote feel about the small, quiet village of Normanton le Heath. The spire of the 13th century church can be seen for miles around across the predominantly flat terrain. Look out for the gargoyles at the top of the west tower.

Normanton le Heath church

4. At a public footpath sign by the church turn left through a gate, walk along the left edge of the churchyard and climb a stile. Continue along the left edge of a field, descending into a dip, crossing a footbridge and heading up again. Climb a stile in the corner, keep ahead through an area of scrub and trees and bear slightly right across grass to another stile. After climbing it, bear right across the next field and in the corner go through a hedge gap onto a road.

Cross over, walk across the verge, climb a waymarked stile and keep ahead diagonally across a field to a waymarked post by a solitary tree. The tree will not be solitary for much longer as the adjoining fields are part of the Diamond Jubilee Wood project and some of the new plantations are already in existence. Beyond the tree continue by a hedge on the left and follow a clear wide track along the left edge of a succession of fields, going through a series of hedge gaps. In the corner of the last of these fields, continue through bushes to climb a stile, cross a footbridge and turn left along the left edge of the next field. At the next waymarked post where the path forks, take the path on the right, continue across the field, go through a gap on the far side and keep ahead by the right field edge to emerge, via a gate, onto a road. Turn left downhill and then head up again.

5. At a public byway sign (this is on the left side of the road), turn right onto a track. Keep along it for just over ½ mile (800m), later heading uphill, and just before reaching the top, turn right beside a gate, at a National Forest Way sign. Walk along a track, go through a gate and keep ahead to join a tarmac track. The track heads gently uphill back to the car park.

Noon Column sculpture in Sence Valley Forest Park

WALK 18
Home of the Nine Day Queen:
Bradgate Park and Swithland Wood

This is a classic walk of superb and varied scenery that takes you through a medieval deer park, a beautiful area of woodland and a picturesque village with an old church and thatched cottages. From the higher points there are outstanding views over Charnwood Forest and the surrounding Leicestershire countryside. Within the park are the atmospheric remains of Bradgate House, home of Lady Jane Grey, the 'Nine Day Queen'.

Distance	5 miles (8 km)
Approx. time	2½ hours
Starting point	Newtown Linford, entrance to Bradgate Park, grid ref SK524098
Parking	Bradgate Park
Terrain	Clear paths and tracks through parkland, woodland and across fields, modest ascents and descents
Refreshments	Pubs and cafes at Newtown Linford; cafe at information centre in Bradgate Park
Public transport	Buses from Leicester, Coalville and Loughborough
Map	OS Explorer 246 (Loughborough)

The Walk

For centuries Newtown Linford was part of the Bradgate Estate. It is an attractive village with a number of thatched and slate-roofed cottages. The church, situated at the gates of the park, was originally a small and simple structure but was enlarged towards the end of the 19th century when the village started to expand.

1. Begin by going through the gates into Bradgate Park and walk along the tarmac track beside the little River Lin. After about ¾ mile (1.2 km) you pass the remains of Bradgate House on the left and a little further on Bradgate Park Visitor Centre and Cropston Reservoir on the right.

Newtown Linford church

In 1928 the current owner, Charles Bennion, presented Bradgate Park to the people of Leicester and Leicestershire as an area of public recreation and enjoyment. Given its proximity to Leicester – only about six miles away – and its herds of deer, it is an extremely popular spot, especially on fine weekends and bank holidays. This rare example of a largely unaltered and unspoilt medieval deer park was carved out of Charnwood Forest in the 13th century and mainly comprises heathland, grassland and bracken dotted with some magnificent ancient oaks and outcrops of granite. The latter give it a rugged appearance which contrasts strongly with the more usual gentler landscapes of Leicestershire.

Ruins of Bradgate House

For most of its history the park was owned by the Grey family and around 1499 Sir Thomas Grey, Marquis of Dorset, began the building of the house, whose redbrick ruins can be seen. Its chief claim to fame is that it was the home of Lady Jane Grey, queen for just nine days in 1553. She was the unwilling figurehead of an unsuccessful attempt by Protestant nobles to prevent the Catholic Mary Tudor from becoming queen on the death of her half brother Edward VI. The unfortunate girl paid the price by being subsequently executed. In 1740 Bradgate House was abandoned by the Greys, after which it fell into disrepair.

Deer in Bradgate Park

At the far end of the park go through gates onto a road.

2. Turn right and at a public footpath sign, turn left over a stile and walk diagonally across a field. Go through a gate in the far corner, keep in the same direction across the next field and go through a kissing gate in the corner. Keep ahead along an enclosed path, go through another kissing gate and turn left along a track. At a fork take the left hand blue-waymarked path,

Ancient trees are dotted around Bradgate Park

go through a gate and continue along the tree-lined path, later heading across open country to a T-junction. Turn left and the path shortly enters Swithland Wood.

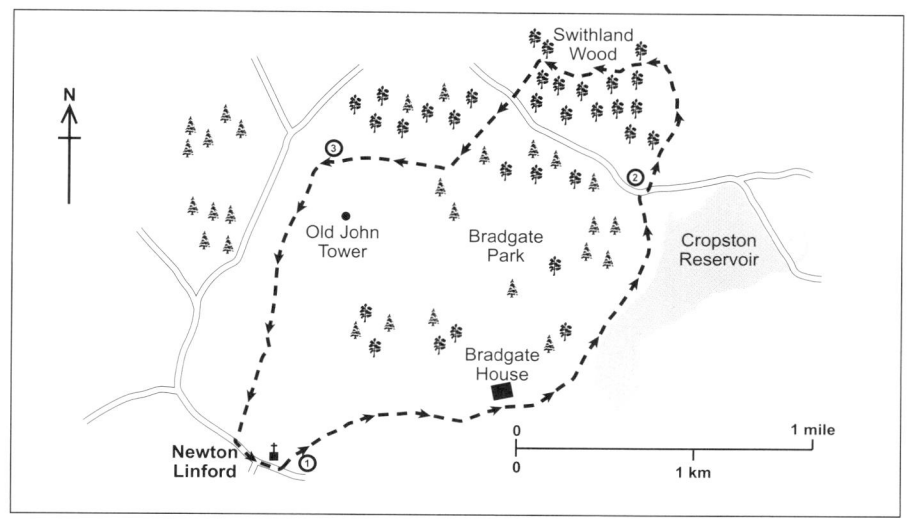

Swithland Wood, a surviving remnant of Charnwood Forest, is a beautiful area of mixed woodland, mainly comprising oak, ash, lime, birch, alder and holly. Like Bradgate Park it was given to the city of Leicester. The remains of quarry workings in the wood are an indication that Swithland slate was much prized locally as a roofing material.

Keep ahead through the trees, turn left at a junction of paths and at the next public bridleway sign, turn right and head uphill. Keep on the main path all the time and eventually you go through a gate on the edge of the wood. Turn left onto an enclosed track, heading gently downhill, and go through a gate onto a road. Cross over, climb the stile opposite and continue gently uphill along a track, part of the National Forest Way. After climbing a stile, turn right and continue steadily uphill along an enclosed path bedside the boundary wall of Bradgate Park on the left, going through two gates before emerging onto a broad track.

3. Turn left through a kissing gate to re-enter the park and ahead is Old John Tower. The route continues to the right but a short detour to the tower is well worth the effort for the superb view.

Old John Tower is a folly, built by a member of the Grey family in 1784. The views from here are both extensive and magnificent.

Return to the kissing gate and turn left onto a path that keeps alongside the park wall on the right, curving gradually left and heading gently downhill. Old John Tower and the war memorial to the Leicestershire Regiment can be seen to the left and there are fine views to the right over the wooded slopes of Charnwood Forest. When you are in line with a clump of trees over to the left (Elder Plantation), turn right through a kissing gate in the boundary wall and walk along the right edge of a field. Bear right to go through a kissing gate in the corner, continue downhill along the right edge of the next field, go through another kissing gate at the bottom and keep ahead to a road. Turn left through Newtown Linford, passing a number of picturesque thatched cottages, and at a sign to Bradgate Park, turn left to return to the car park.

WALK 19
Views across the Water:
Thornton Reservoir and Stanton under Bardon

As with several other walks in this guide, it takes quite an effort of the imagination to visualise the surrounding pleasant landscape of green fields, new plantations and reservoir as being scarred by coal mines and pit heaps but this was the case until fairly recently. The route takes in a number of young woods planted through The National Forest project and there are a series of fine views both across Thornton Reservoir and over the Leicestershire countryside.

Distance	5 miles (8 km)
Approx. time	2½ hours
Starting point	Thornton Reservoir, grid ref SK471075
Parking	Severn Trent car park at Thornton Reservoir
Terrain	Apart from waterside paths at the start and finish, most of the walking is along field and woodland paths with some fairly gentle gradients
Refreshments	Pubs at Thornton, garden centre cafe by car park entrance, pub at Stanton under Bardon
Public transport	Buses from Leicester and Coalville
Map	OS Explorer 245 (The National Forest)

The Walk

Unlike Staunton Harold, the 75 acre Thornton Reservoir has been in existence for a long time. It was constructed in 1854 but only made available to the general public in 1997. Since then it has become a popular centre for birdwatchers, anglers, cyclists and walkers.

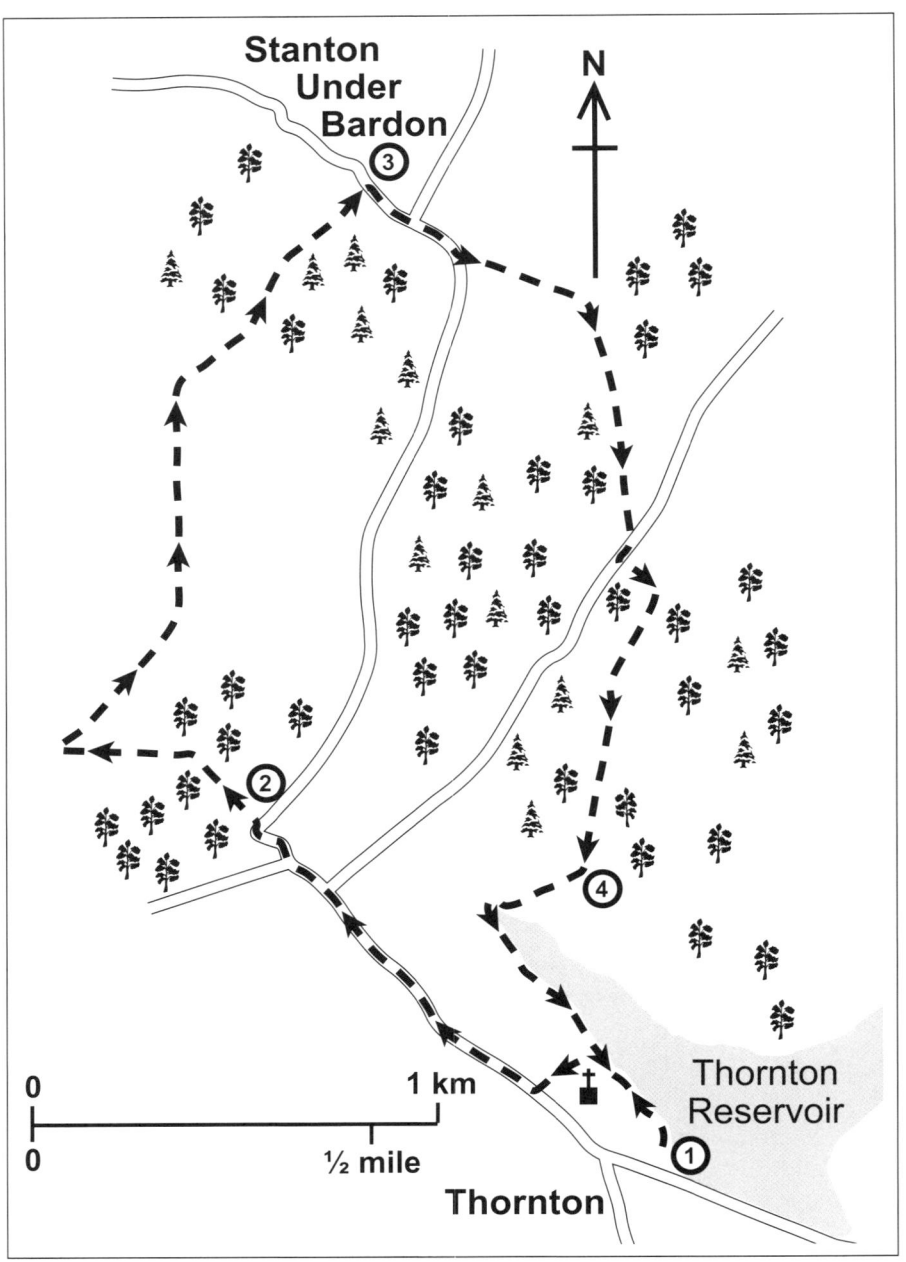

Looking across Thornton Reservoir

1. Facing the reservoir, turn left along the tarmac path beside it, passing the information centre and toilet block. Shortly after going through a kissing gate turn left, at a public footpath sign, and head uphill along a path which bends right and continues along the right edge of Thornton churchyard. Pass beside the lych gate and keep ahead to a T-junction in Thornton village.

Thornton was originally an agricultural settlement on the fringes of Charnwood Forest and later became a mining village. The fine 13th century church has an impressive spire.

Turn right and where the main road bends left, keep ahead along Stanton Lane.

2. Where the lane bends right, climb the stile in front and walk along a path through the young woodland of Thornton Plantation, planted in 1998. The path curves left to a stile. Climb it and walk across a field – the village of Bagworth can be seen on the ridge ahead – to a footpath post on the far

side. At this point turn sharp right and follow a path gently uphill across the same field, making for the far left hand corner. Go through a wide hedge gap and turn left along the left edge of the next field, keeping in line with the electricity pylons. At a waymarked stile by another wide hedge gap the path divides. Take the right hand path, heading diagonally across the field to a stile. Climb it and turn left along the left edge of another area of recently planted woodland.

This new wood, planted as recently as 2002-03, is called Partings Wood and the name has an interesting derivation. It is situated approximately half way between the villages of Thornton and Stanton under Bardon and courting couples allegedly used to part here when walking each other home.

New plantations near Thornton

Turn right at the corner of the wood to continue along its right edge and turn left over a stile. Head downhill across a field to a stile, climb it and go through the squeezer stile immediately in front onto a lane.

3. Turn right and the first lane on the left leads uphill into Stanton under Bardon if you want to visit the village and pub.

As its name indicates Stanton is situated below Bardon Hill, which at 912 feet (278m) is the highest hill in Leicestershire. It was a quarrying village and the hill has been quarried for its distinctive greenish rock, a kind of granite, since as early as 1622.

Otherwise the route continues ahead along the lane to where it bends right. At this point keep ahead over a stile and walk along the left edge of a field. In the corner turn right to continue along the edge and at the next field corner, climb a stile and follow the path through a plantation, part of Partings Wood again. At the corner of the wood, cross a footbridge, keep ahead and go through a gate onto a road. Turn right and at a public footpath sign, turn left through a hedge gap and walk along the left edge of the National Forest plantation of Ashley's Wood. Turn right at a waymarked post to continue through the trees, climb a stile – here leaving the wood – and keep along the right edge of a field. Climb a stile just to the left of the corner and continue in a straight line gently downhill through Browns Wood. Look out for where you turn left over a footbridge at a yellow waymarked post, turn right and at a fork immediately ahead, take the left hand path. Climb a stile on the edge of the trees – there is a fine view ahead of the reservoir and spire of Thornton church – turn right along a right field edge and go through a kissing gate onto a track.

4. Turn right and cross an outlet stream at the end of the reservoir. The track curves left and continues beside the water back to the start.

WALK 20
Death of a King:
Bosworth Battlefield

Starting from the Heritage Centre on top of Ambion Hill, a superb viewpoint, most of the route is across what has traditionally been accepted as the site of the Battle of Bosworth and the first part of it follows a well-signed Battle Trail with regular information boards. Although the terrain has changed much since the time of the battle in 1485 – the most obvious additions are the railway, canal and Ambion Wood – Bosworth is one of the best preserved battle sites in England and it is still possible, with a little imagination, to follow the course of the conflict.

Distance	3 miles (4.8 km)
Approx. time	2 hours
Starting point	Bosworth Battlefield Heritage Centre, signposted from A447 and other roads near Market Bosworth, grid ref SK402001
Parking	Bosworth Battlefield
Terrain	Easy walking along mostly well-surfaced paths and a canal towpath
Refreshments	Cafe at Heritage Centre, cafe at Shenton station, canalside cafe at Sutton Wharf
Public transport	None
Map	OS Explorer 232 (Nuneaton & Tamworth)

The Walk

By any criteria Bosworth ranks as one of the most significant battles in English history. It was virtually the final battle in the long Wars of the Roses, ushered in the powerful Tudor dynasty and is widely regarded as marking the end of the Middle Ages. It was also the last occasion on which an English king was killed in battle. It was fought on 22 August 1485 between Richard III and Henry Tudor and at stake was the throne of England.

Richard III had come to the throne two years before in highly dubious circumstances. In that year his brother Edward IV died at an early age and his successor, Edward V, was a boy of only 12. Richard, then Duke of Gloucester and the young king's uncle, acted as regent and arranged for Edward and his younger brother, Richard Duke of York, to be conveyed to the Tower of London. Richard then had himself crowned king and the two 'Princes in the Tower' later mysteriously disappeared. Not surprisingly such action aroused much hostility and discontent among the nobility and Henry Tudor Earl of Richmond, a Welshman and currently in exile in France, became the focal point of opposition to Richard.

Henry landed in Pembrokeshire on 7 August 1485 and marched across Wales and into the Midlands. Richard was based at Nottingham Castle. He moved to Leicester and the two armies met near Market Bosworth. Richard had the advantage of occupying the top of Ambion Hill, the starting point of the walk, and had a larger and more experienced army but, because of his widespread unpopularity, some of his supporters were lukewarm. The turning point in the battle came when the powerful Stanleys threw their 4,000 troops behind Henry. After fierce fighting, Richard was defeated and killed and Henry Tudor ascended the throne as Henry VII, the first of the Tudor monarchs.

Recent archaeological discoveries have now indicated that, although Richard III's army gathered on Ambion Hill at the start of the battle, the likeliest site where the bulk of the fighting took place was on low lying ground about two miles to the south in the vicinity of the villages of Dadlington and Stoke Golding. This means that the association of some of the places on or around the hill with the battle may no longer apply. All this is explained in great depth at the Heritage Centre but in no way do these changes and debates about the exact site, which are still ongoing, detract from either the scenic or historical appeal of this walk. If anything it only makes it more absorbing and, although a short walk, you need to allow plenty of time in order to get the most out of your visit.

As well as dealing with these latest reinterpretations of the battle site, the Heritage Centre provides plenty of information about the background to Bosworth, the claims to the throne of the two main protagonists, the course and consequences of the battle and much more, making use of interactive models. There is also a wide variety of books and gifts, plus refreshment facilities.

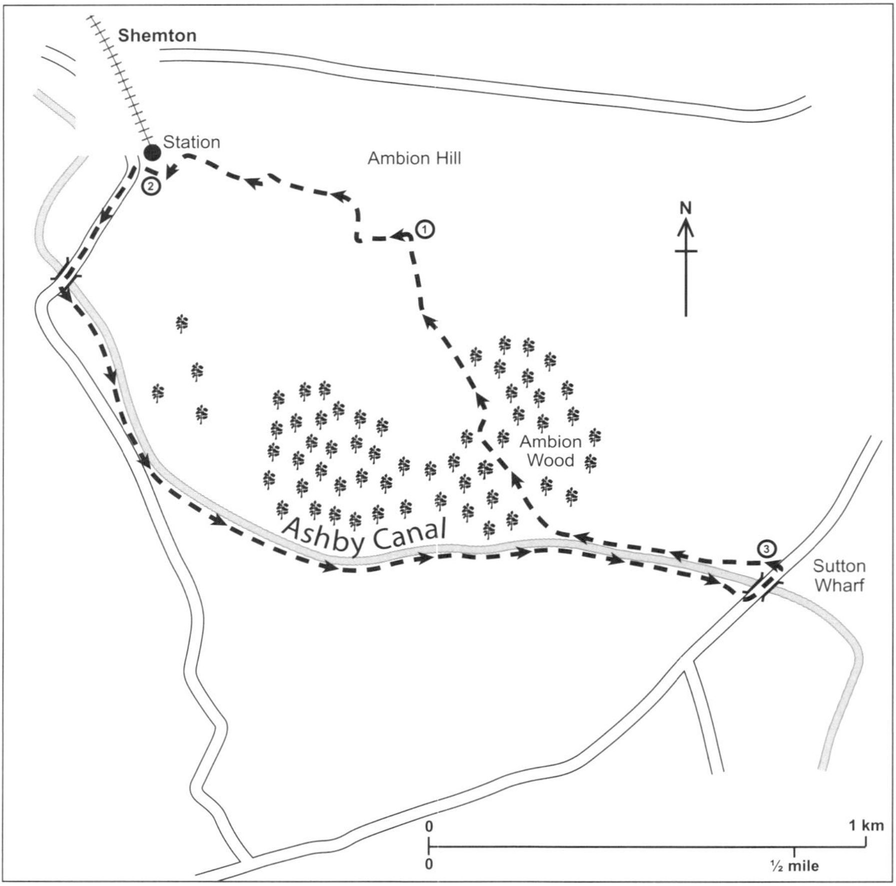

1. Start at the entrance to the Heritage Centre by turning left and left again beside the building and head across to a Battle of Bosworth Trail information board. Bear left to join a well-surfaced path and go through a hedge gap in the field corner to King Richard's Well.

King Richard's Well

Richard III is supposed to have slaked his thirst from the spring here during the battle. It is now topped by a stone pyramid.

Go back through the hedge gap and turn left uphill, making your way to a group of flags seen ahead. A few yards to the right of these is the Memorial Sundial.

This is a recent and very attractive development, built here to commemorate all those killed in the battle in 1485. It is in the shape of a circle and among its features are three thrones – one each for Richard III, Henry Tudor and Lord Stanley – information plaques and a display of rose bushes representing the Wars of the Roses.

Memorial Sundial at the site of the Battle of Bosworth

From the garden keep ahead to a fence gap – there is a yellow-waymarked post – on the crest of the hill. Despite its modest height, 354 feet (120m), Ambion Hill is a fine vantage point and from here there are grand views over open and gently undulating country looking towards Market Bosworth. Go through the gap

View from Ambion Hill

and the path curves left and heads downhill. At the bottom go through two gates in quick succession and keep ahead to Shenton station.

The station is one of the termini on the Battlefield Line. The trains, both steam-hauled and diesel, run from here to Shackerstone where there is a museum, shop and cafe.

Cross the railway line and bear right across the station car park to a road.

2. Turn left and after crossing a canal bridge, turn sharp left (almost doubling back) along an enclosed path to the canal. Turn right along the towpath.

The Ashby Canal was built between 1794 and 1804 and linked the coal mines around Moira and Ashby with the Coventry Canal near Nuneaton. It declined after the coming of the railways and this, coupled with instability caused by mining subsidence, led to its closure in the 1940s. Some of the northern industrial part has disappeared but this southerly, more agricultural section has survived and is a popular recreational amenity, passing through much unspoilt and pleasant countryside.

Ashby Canal

Now comes a very attractive stretch of canalside walking to Sutton Wharf, a distance of 1¼ miles (2 km). At Bridge 34 climb steps onto the road and turn left over the bridge.

3. Turn left again through a gate into Sutton Wharf car park and continue along the other side of the canal. Go through a kissing gate and keep ahead to enter Ambion Wood.

Although it occupies part of the battle site, Ambion Wood did not exist in 1485. The terrain then comprised open grassy slopes.

The path curves right through the trees to a kissing gate on the edge of the wood. Go through, walk across a field, go through another kissing gate and keep ahead to the start.

Also from Sigma Leisure:

Walks in the Midlands Countryside
around Birmingham and the Black Country: Tracing the Journeys of a 19th Century Writer
Brian Conduit

In 1865 Elihu Burritt, a notable American peace and anti-slavery activist, was appointed the United States consul in Birmingham, at the time a rapidly growing manufacturing city and centre of a major industrial area. He travelling extensively throughout the Midlands. These 20 walks take you through areas of the Midlands which, 150 years since Burritt walked this way, still contain some of the most varied, beautiful and interesting landscapes and some of the finest old towns and villages in the country.
£8.99

Heart of England Way
102 miles of linear walk or 225 miles of 32 linked circular walks
Stephen J Cross

A book both for the long distance and the leisure walker, The Heart of England Way, and 32 circular walks, takes the walker on a journey slicing through the quieter areas of midland, shire, countryside; from the north edge of Cannock Chase, to Bourton on the Water; providing a fascinating view through the back door of the regions history, people, buildings and landscape.
£8.99

All of our books are all available on-line at **www.sigmapress.co.uk** or through booksellers. For a free catalogue, please contact:

Sigma Leisure, Stobart House, Pontyclerc, Penybanc Road, Ammanford, Carmarthenshire SA18 3HP
Tel: 01269 593100 Fax: 01269 596116

info@sigmapress.co.uk www.sigmapress.co.uk